A KEY TO
POTTERY AND GLASS

A KEY TO
POTTERY AND GLASS

BY

BERNARD RACKHAM, C.B., F.S.A.

Formerly Keeper of the Department of Ceramics
Victoria and Albert Museum

BLACKIE & SON LIMITED
LONDON AND GLASGOW

BLACKIE & SON LIMITED
50 Old Bailey, London
17 Stanhope Street, Glasgow
BLACKIE & SON (INDIA) LIMITED
Warwick House, Fort Street, Bombay
BLACKIE & SON (CANADA) LIMITED
Toronto

First published 1940

Printed in Great Britain by Blackie & Son, Ltd., Glasgow

PREFACE

IN conformity with the plan of the series to which it belongs, this book is not meant for the expert. It is addressed rather to those with little or no knowledge of the subject whose curiosity stirs in them a wish to understand something of the nature and antecedents of articles they use in daily life, particularly of articles made in two kinds of material of such beauty and attractiveness as may and should belong to pottery and glass. Most of its readers are likely to be interested chiefly in English wares; the book is accordingly designed to show how the china and glass, efficient for their purpose and perfect in workmanship, which we expect as a matter of course to be able to obtain for domestic use, are the culmination of many strains of development traceable through long ages to the most various and widely distant origins. So short a volume is not intended to serve, like an encyclopædia, as a work of reference; names of craftsmen, dates, and minor technical details have accordingly been to a large extent left out as an encumbrance in what it is hoped will be found a readable general survey. Those whose interest the book succeeds in stimulating may be referred, amongst other works, to the handbooks on special aspects of the two subjects published at moderate prices by the two great national museums. These handbooks will be found to contain adequate bibliographies of the authorities on which they are based and from which a large part of the facts recorded in this short volume are also derived. I should like to record my indebtedness in particular, as regards the earlier section of the book, to the writings of my friend, Mr. R. L. Hobson, lately of the British Museum; I have found very useful also a little book by Mr. H. S. Harrison with the modest title *Pots and Pans* (Howe, London, 1928), which can be recommended with confidence to those whose interest is less in the history of pottery than in the manner in which it is made. For glass I have found quite invaluable a work unfortunately not available in translation, *Das Glas* (2nd ed., 1922), by Prof. Robert Schmidt, a handbook published by the Schlossmuseum, Berlin; English glass, however, is there inadequately treated, and for this branch of the subject, in common with all students, I owe very much to the tireless and painstaking researches of another friend, Mr. Francis Buckley. For statements based on recent and, in some cases, not readily accessible publications, I have thought it well to give references in the footnotes.

Finally, I may point out that the all-embracing collections of the British and Victoria and Albert Museums provide unsurpassed material in illustration of my two-fold subject; the specimens exhibited in the Fitzwilliam Museum, Cambridge, and the Royal Scottish Museum, Edinburgh, are also fairly adequate for the purpose. I have to thank the Directors of these museums and of the London Museum, as well as Mr. D. Kelekian and Mrs. L. G. Drummond, for kind permission to reproduce photographs of objects in their several collections. Messrs. Rydbeck & Norström kindly supplied the photograph reproduced on Plate XVI, D.

BERNARD RACKHAM.

NOTE

It is convenient to point out here that detailed descriptions of the objects reproduced in the plates will be found in the list on pp. ix-xii.

CONTENTS

PART ONE—POTTERY

PART TWO—GLASS

LIST OF PLATES

PART I — POTTERY

CHAPTER I

Origins

THE art of the potter is one of the oldest of human handicrafts. How pottery was invented will doubtless never be known, nor when and where the earliest clay pots were made, for they were certainly far too perishable to have survived, like stone implements, till our own time. We may guess that the idea of using pots as containers occurred to some man or, more likely, woman—the potters of primitive races are women—who noticed how rainwater gathered in foot or hoof prints in clayey ground and how clay hardened with the heat of the sun. Rude vessels shaped in plastic clay with the hands were doubtless hardened by drying in the sun long before the much more efficient method of baking with fire was thought of. The shaping of pottery was enormously facilitated by the invention of the potter's wheel, which consists essentially of a small round table on a supporting shaft passing through a larger flywheel; the flywheel may be set in motion by the feet or the disengaged hand of the potter, or as in modern times by a band connecting it with a wheel turned by an assistant or by mechanical power in various forms. Whatever the motive power, the principle remains the same, and by the process known as " throwing " on the wheel a pot can be given a true circular shape far more quickly and easily than by laboriously fashioning the clay with the hands unaided. Other and, in some respects, easier ways of shaping clay vessels, such as moulding and casting, of which more will be said later, were devised as time went on, but none gives such satisfactory results as " throwing ". The fact remains, however, that pots of great beauty and refinement of shape were made in early times—and continue to be made by primitive races in Africa and America—entirely without mechanical aid, unless we class as a machine what is called the " slow wheel ", a flat slab of stone or the base of a broken pot on which the clay could be slowly revolved with one hand, whilst being shaped with the other. Another laborious method, still practised by American Indians and capable in their skilful hands of giving admirable results, is that of building up the walls of a pot by coiling and interlocking snake-like rolls or ropes of clay and afterwards smoothing out the interstices.

Pottery may be divided on a technical basis into three main classes—earthenware, stoneware and porcelain, evolved in that chronological sequence; there are no sharp dividing lines between the three classes, which tend to merge into one another, so that intermediate types have appeared from time to time. Roughly speaking, earthenware and stoneware are made of clay alone, or perhaps with a smaller or greater admixture of silica in the form of sand or ground flints, differing only in the degree of temperature to which they are fired; stoneware is earthenware fired until the particles of clay are fused into a homogeneous mass like stone which cannot be powdered by scraping with a steel blade. Porcelain is the name given to translucent white pottery made by combining clay with various other substances, and is itself divisible according to the nature of its constituents into several classes, of which more will be said when porcelain comes on the scene

in the historical sequence. These various types, cul-
minating in the fine white " china " which we expect
nowadays almost as a matter of course for use at table,
are the outcome of a series of improvements discovered
at intervals over a long range of time. One of these
is, as we have seen, the potter's wheel; glaze is another,
which, with many more, will be dealt with in its place
as the narrative proceeds.

The oldest surviving pottery can be dated back to
the Neolithic period of human culture. It has to be
borne in mind, however, that the Stone Age lasted
in some parts of the world down to a much more
recent time than in others; so that when we speak
of the Neolithic pottery of Egypt or China we are con-
cerned with wares much older than the Neolithic pottery
of northern and western Europe, whilst in America
Neolithic pottery has endured virtually till modern
times.

The earliest wares dug up out of graves in Great
Britain and elsewhere in north-western Europe date
from about the second half of the third millennium
before Christ; they exhibit the characteristics to be
expected of pottery in a primitive stage. The material
is a friable drab or reddish earthenware; the round-
bottomed form which comes most naturally in wares
made entirely by hand was succeeded by beakers and
jars flattened at the base so that they can stand up-
right without support. Decoration of some sort is
almost constant on the wares found in graves, but was
not necessarily so general on those made for ordinary
use. It is of the kind which inevitably suggests itself
in working soft material; it consists, that is, of rec-
tilinear motives—horizontal lines, zigzags, bands or
straight-sided compartments filled with trellis-pattern
—scratched into the surface with the finger-nail or
with a stick, or very commonly in broken dotted lines
produced either by pressing into the clay a twisted cord
or with a notched curved slip or disc of wood or bone

(like a coarsely milled coin). The typical shapes found in the British Isles are the beaker, more or less bell-shaped, the " food-vessel " (fig. 1), and the cinerary urn, the last sometimes as much as thirty inches high, with sides expanding to a high shoulder and short contracted neck in some cases overhung by inward-slanting eaves as the uppermost member. An interesting and, from a decorative point of view, a very effective feature of the " food-vessel " is often a deep groove

Fig. 1.—Early Bronze Age "food-vessel" (British Museum)

interrupted at intervals by an ear or stop which may be pierced to form a loop. Taken as a whole the Stone Age and Bronze Age pottery of the north, though coarse in material and decorated only with the most obvious of patterns by the simplest of methods, proves in its makers a highly developed sense for beauty of form and fitness in decoration.

It is not surprising that refinement makes its appearance first in the lands of the Nile and the Euphrates, in which civilization was born. We have no evidence to suggest how early pottery may first have been made in Egypt; before Egyptian history begins, however, with the first dynasty of kings, towards the end of the

(F 778)

fourth millennium B.C. we find pottery being made which, although still shaped by hand unaided (the wheel being a later invention), shows by its great refinement of shape and finish that it must have had a long ancestry tracing back to rude, primitive types now lost. This pre-dynastic pottery is of two classes. In one there is no decoration, but the surface is hard and burnished smooth; it is either bright red all over, from a coating of hæmatite (iron ore), or in some cases black, or black in the upper part only, this change of colour having been effected, it is supposed, by partially burying

Fig. 2.—Pre-dynastic Egyptian pot

the pot during firing in the ashes of the furnace so that, in the portion thus covered, the full oxidation which produces the red colour could not take place. The shapes of this plain red or black ware are of extraordinary grace and beauty; a slender oviform with flat base and plain truncation at the mouth is typical. The wares of the second class are distinguished by their decoration, either linear, derived from basketwork, as in certain black wares with scratched designs with white clay rubbed into them, or representational, painted either in white on a red ground or in red on buff; amongst these latter designs we find crudely drawn men, animals and boats, but of greater æsthetic merit is a more or less regular diaper of shell-like coils harmonizing admirably with the often distinguished shapes of the vessels (fig. 2). An egg-shaped jar with flat base and another of depressed globular form rounded at the bottom, both provided with two small pierced handles like a tubular bead, set horizontally, just above the greatest diameter, are forms common to both types of decorated ware; they have their precise analogies in the contemporary vessels made by drilling out of several varieties of stone—the buff earthenware jars are indeed sometimes mottled with red to imitate the markings of breccia. In early dynastic times, as the result of increased skill in making vases of stone and perhaps also of the introduction of metal-working, there was a falling off in the quality of Egyptian pottery, but this was only temporary, and unglazed earthenware of good form continued to be made under the rule of later dynasties. It is, however, to the invention of glaze, in other words, of glass (compare p. 126), that Egypt owes its outstanding position in the history of pottery. This development was a very important step in advance, as a glaze if rightly constituted greatly increases the usefulness of pottery as a container for liquids by making it non-porous and easy to keep clean. It is necessary only to reflect on the inconvenience that would be caused in modern life if instead of well-glazed china we had nothing better for use than earthenware like that of flower-pots and chimney-pots.

By the introduction of glaze and subsequent developments Ancient Egypt has its place at the head of the stream which we shall have to follow in the chapter on Near-Eastern pottery. Here we can only mention briefly other classes of unglazed earthenware made in pre-Christian times in the Near East. Many such types belong to the civilizations of the lower Euphrates valley of which recent excavations have so greatly extended our knowledge. Most remarkable of these are the buff earthenware jars and beakers attributed to the fourth millennium before Christ, found in the lowest stratum of the ruins of Susa, in Elam, the land which, through the conquest of its early inhabitants by Aryan invaders from the north, was later to become part of what we know as Persia; these are painted in purplish black with designs geometrical in effect but found on close inspection to comprise highly stylized animals and birds—goats, for instance, with horns rendered as enormous coils out of all proportion to their bodies, or ostriches in Indian file looking like rows of spots combined with " pot-hooks and hangers ". Analogous wares have been found by Sir Leonard Woolley at " Ur of the Chaldees ", the royal city of Sumer, as well as later types. This explorer's most recent excavations, at Atchana near Antioch, have proved that fine painted pottery was made in early times in Syria also; good examples are two jars attributed to the second millennium B.C., with bird and scroll designs in white on a red ground, which are amongst his latest finds.[1] From these early Oriental wares we shall now turn to those of the classic lands of antiquity, which since the time of their first re-discovery have been one of the chief influences on the potter's art.

[1] *The Antiquaries' Journal*, XIX, 1939, pl. XV.

CHAPTER II

Greece and Rome

THE wares which by common consent are known collectively as "Greek vases" constitute a phenomenon virtually without a parallel; in their importance as historical documents, if not in their peculiar standing as works of art, they surpass the nearest analogies offered by the pottery of later times such as the *minai* ware of Persia, Chinese porcelain, or Italian maiolica. Beginning like many other ancient wares as decorated pottery, they became at their best vehicles for graphic composition and draughtsmanship of the highest order and, at the same time, an invaluable repertory of illustrations bearing on the literature and life of one of the world's greatest civilizations.

The earliest pottery found on Greek soil is not dissimilar in technique to Neolithic wares from other Mediterranean countries; bowls and cups often of very beautiful shape were made by hand without the aid of a wheel, sometimes burnished to a fine glossy black or red surface and ornamented with incised linear patterns. It was only when painting in earthy pigments was discovered as a method of decoration that the seeds were sown from which sprang the splendid harvest of later ages.

Painted pottery was made by the early inhabitants of Greece concurrently both on the mainland, in the kingdoms which were to hand down to posterity legends of the heroic rulers of Mycenæ and Argos, and in many of the islands of the Ægean Sea, but nowhere was the art brought to such perfection as in Crete. Only in recent decades has exploration laid bare the remains of the wonderful culture which has received its name from Minos, famed in Greek legend for his Labyrinth and its monstrous inmate, half man, half bull. We now know that whilst this great Cretan kingdom endured, in the Bronze Age of the Greek world, lasting from about 3000 to about 1200 B.C., the island was the seat of a great art revealing itself in architecture, wall-painting, metalwork in bronze and gold, stone-carving, and not least in painted pottery.

In the Cretan wares made during the periods which are known to archæologists as Early, Middle and Late Minoan we have evidence for the first time on Greek territory of the use of the potter's wheel. For a time there is little progress in form from the unsophisticated shapes of the hand-made Neolithic pottery, but an obviously distinctive feature is the use of painted decoration. At first, it is true, the introduction of metal-working into Crete involved a decline in the art of the potter, but revival came in due course, with this notable advance in technique. In the earliest stages, brown earthy pigment was used for painting geometrical designs on the natural buff earthenware surface, and later the reverse effect was obtained by the employment of white pigment over a ground of black " slip " with which the surface had previously been overlaid. (This brings for the first time to our notice a technical term of frequent occurrence in books on pottery; "slip" is clay, of any colour but most often white, brought to the consistency of cream by mixing with water, and used either as a surface dressing or as a medium of decoration.)

In the Middle Minoan period an almost monumental sense of form is apparent, combined with magnificent painted designs now no longer merely linear or geometrical but derived from nature and handled with skilful stylization as elements in ordered pattern. It is characteristic of a seafaring people that they drew almost exclusively on marine life—seaweed, fishes, molluscs, and conspicuously the octopus. For rendering these themes a wide range of colours was brought into play, from black to brown, red, buff and white. It is, perhaps, an indication of a weakened artistic sense that in the beginning of what is known as the Late Minoan age, that is, some 1600 years before Christ, these marine and other natural motives came to be treated in a naturalistic way—still, it is true, with a good feeling for their right placing on the surface in relation to the shapes of the vessels; an octopus, for instance, is shown gracefully waving its tentacles in pursuit of small shell-fishes amongst branching seaweeds. In the last phase before the decline of the Cretan civilization came about there was a return to a more formal and more strictly decorative rendering; the results, applied to shapes of elegant refinement, are sometimes of exquisite beauty, although lacking the impressive power of the earlier styles. As something quite exceptional must be mentioned finally the appearance, about the end of the Middle Minoan period, of siliceous glazes coloured blue and purple with copper and manganese; this technique was introduced from Egypt (compare p. 59) and had no lasting effect on Greek pottery.

Cretan painted pottery stands pre-eminent amongst the wares of the Greek region in these early times, before the advent from the north of the tribes who were to be the founders of the Greece to which the world owes so much. But kindred if generally inferior pottery was made at the same time both on the mainland of the Peloponnesus and in several of the Ægean Islands. To discuss such local variations as they present would take us beyond the scope of a general survey.

The period in which the early Ægean civilization was overthrown, in some regions perhaps in catastrophic downfall, in most more probably by gradual infiltration, before the advance of the Greek invaders from the

north, was one of general decline in the arts, including
pottery. A revival came about with the slow growth
of a new culture in the Greek " Middle Ages " (as the
succeeding period has been called), and in the ninth
and eighth centuries B.C. we find the earliest " Greek
Vases " proper. Painted wares, sometimes of enormous
size, appear in shapes such as the two-handled wine-
jar or *amphora*, which anticipate some of the familiar
vases of the classical age. The decoration is stiff and
formal, with none of the spontaneous grace of the best
early Cretan painted wares; it consists in general of
tedious geometrical patterns, notably the meander or
key pattern, displayed row upon row in horizontal
zones encircling the body and neck. On the more
important vases human figures, birds and animals are
introduced on a small scale amongst these geometrical
motives, but themselves reduced as a rule to severely
geometrical silhouettes. Foremost amongst these
geometrical wares are the products of the Ceramicus,
the famous potter's quarter outside the Dipylon
(" Double Gate ") of Athens, which city thus makes its
first appearance on the stage on which it was afterwards to play so splendid a role. The style was not,
however, confined to Athens, and on the outskirts of
the Greek world it lingered in a modified form when
it had been generally superseded; the jars, bottles and
bowls in buff or bright red earthenware, painted in
dark brown solely or chiefly with groups of concentric
circles, which were made as late as the sixth century B.C.
in Cyprus, have been dug up and brought in such numbers
to Great Britain and America that they are to be found
amongst the ceramic collections of many museums.

A more interesting repertory of decorative themes
came to the knowledge of the Greek potters when
trading contacts with the East were formed as a result
of the foundation of the Ionian Greek colonies on the
eastern shores of the Ægean, in Asia Minor. Such
Oriental influences naturally made themselves felt first

in Ionia itself and in Rhodes and other adjacent islands, as may be seen in the pottery there made. What may be termed the home port to which the Oriental exports were carried, either direct or by way of these Ionian cities, was Corinth, and it became the chief seat of manufacture of these orientalizing wares, from which they were distributed overseas even as far as Italy, Africa, and the Greek colonies in the Crimea. The characteristics of the Corinthian and kindred wares of the seventh and sixth centures are a buff " body ", painting in black, purplish red and white, and designs either of animals, birds, and supernatural creatures such as sphinxes and harpies arranged in horizontal rows (sometimes several on a single vase), or of palmettes or lotus-flowers, in all of which a deriva-tion from Eastern art can be recognized (Plate I, B). Details of the figures or other designs are incised through the pigment with a pointed instrument. The interspaces are thickly sprinkled with rosettes or other small ornaments, so that no part of the surface appears blank, the effect being so strongly suggestive of carpets or embroidered fabrics as to indicate that imported textiles were the carriers of these notions from further east. The commonest but artistically least important of the Corinthian pots are the small footless oil-flasks (*lekythi*), in which the cosmetics for which Corinth was also famous were traded throughout the civilized world.

On the later examples of Corinthian vases human figures as well as animals begin to make their appear-ance. The potters of Athens, now rapidly rising in importance under good government in the sixth century, adopted and improved upon the Corinthian style. On their wares the Oriental animals and plants soon began to yield place to human figures, which had never disappeared from Attic vases since the " geo-metrical " period. A famous example of the new figure-painting is the greater *krater* or jar for mixing wine and water known from the name of its finder

PLATE I

A. " Black-figure " *amphora*, Attic (British Museum)
(Page 13)

B. Bowl, Ionian (Victoria and Albert Museum)
(Page 12)

as the " François Vase " and preserved at Florence.
Its sides are clothed with no less than six friezes crowded
with scenes from mythology—hunters and charioteers,
horsemen, warriors and women—painted with delicate
precision and perfect mastery of technique in black
on the burnished red surface. We have here the beginnings of the " black-figure " style of vase-painting—
painting, that is to say, in which the figures are done
in black glaze-pigment in silhouette on the red ground
(Plate I, A); details, as on the Corinthian vases, are
incised through the pigment right into the " body " of
the ware, and sometimes further aided with purple and
white pigments (the latter especially for women, to
distinguish their paler complexion from that of the
swarthy men). At a date about the end of the sixth
century " black-figure " painting yielded to " red-
figure ", in which the ground was covered with black
pigment and the figures and accessories were left in
reserve to show red; details were now painted in fine
black lines instead of being engraved, and, in the
work of the finest period, auxiliary pigments were
given up, only to be resumed and elaborated when
vase-painting was again in decline. For a time the
two styles ran concurrently, occasionally being employed by a single artist for compositions on one and
the same piece—on opposite sides of an *amphora*,
for instance, or inside and outside a drinking-cup; nor
was the " black-figure " style entirely abandoned;
it was employed till much later on certain funeral
vases for which an archaic manner was deliberately
chosen for solemnity of effect.

We are now in the presence of a great art, one of
several practised at Athens in the fifth century before
Christ. But fastidious devotees of pottery may rightly
object that it is rather a great graphic art than a high
form of the ceramic or plastic art. Content with a
lightly fired, porous " body ", the Athenians did not
attempt any daring adventures with high tempera-

tures, like the Chinese or the stoneware and porcelain potters of modern Europe; though their black pigment is in the nature of a glaze (the constitution of which continues to be somewhat puzzling to technicians), they knew nothing of the splendid glazes stained with metallic oxides invented by the Egyptians and learnt from them in the past, as a brief episode (as we have seen), by the Cretans, and in later ages by generations of Syrian and Persian potters. They worked their clay to such a fine consistency that they were able to give to their wares, by the use of polishing tools at a second turning on the wheel after they had been allowed to dry and harden, a smooth surface no less suited than parchment or paper to receive the most subtle and delicate touches of a fine brush. Their chosen shapes— the *amphora* for storing and the *œnochoe* for pouring wine, the *hydria* for fetching water from the fountain, the shallow *kylix* demanding of the drinker a steadier hand than even the modern champagne-glass—these and many another seem by the graceful perfection of their proportions and outline, and the sharp angles between their members, to show that, in their making, emulation of vessels in bronze or silver was the constant aim; the sturdy jars and ewers of earlier Greek potters certainly proclaim in a more satisfying way their origin in a soft plastic material pressed and guided into shape by unaided human hands. But Greek vases, and particularly the Attic vases of the austere style prevalent in the first half of the fifth century, cannot fail by their paintings to excite the admiration of all lovers of art. For a short period crowded compositions and accessory decorations, such as palmettes and borders of meander, were avoided by some of the best painters in favour of single figures or a pair of figures severely isolated in silhouette on the plain black ground, with no more than a short supporting strip of formal ornament or perhaps a simple line to obviate an effect of floating in space. Later more and more of

the surface is occupied by friezes of figures and pictorial scenes with many participators, in ever increasing elaboration; a schematic treatment of profile,
eyes and muscles, and folds of drapery was superseded
as the fifth century wore on, by an ever nearer approach
to a naturalistic rendering in which foreshortening and
some degree of perspective were skilfully employed.
Sincerity and directness of appeal were lost in a fussy
effort to crowd as much as possible into the picture.
A similar elaboration is shown in the palmettes and
other ornament enlisted to fill subsidiary spaces.

In their choice of subjects the Athenian vase-painters
cover almost every conceivable aspect of social life,
the destiny of the soul after death, and the myths of
gods and heroes handed down by Homer and other
poets. In the earlier and later periods alike we find
much repetition of stereotyped designs, and the evidence
of literature seems to show that some of the compositions are based on fresco and panel paintings; they
have in fact the same relation to the works of Polygno-
tus and Zeuxis as the figure-paintings on Italian
maiolica or eighteenth-century porcelain to those of
Raphael, Watteau or Boucher. But there can be little
doubt that some at least of the vase-paintings by the
great masters of the art are original compositions;
the boy with a hare in the British Museum, the *dis-
cobolus* at South Kensington (Plate II, B), or the girl
spinning a top on a cup at Brussels, and countless
others that could be named, are unmistakably spontaneous sketches of incidents in everyday life, and
many of the mythological designs have no less the
appearance of originality.

The plastic nature of clay has often tempted potters
to make vessels in human or animal form, and the
Greeks were no exception. Amongst the finest Attic
vases, from the point of view of technical perfection,
are the drinking-cups of the type called *rhyton*, made to
be emptied at a single draught, which are moulded in the

shape of animals' or human heads; oil-flasks were also
similarly moulded as figures or even whole groups, and
sometimes a dramatic incident is thus represented in
the round, as in the case of a vase in the Fitzwilliam
Museum, Cambridge, in the form of a negro being
seized by a crocodile. In these relief-moulded wares
we have an anticipation of the technique which was
in Roman times to supplant painting as a method of
decorating pottery. Another exception to the normal
" red-figure " technique is that of the bottles (*lekythi*)
used at Athens to contain offerings at tombs and made
specially for this purpose; in these the greater part
of the surface was prepared with a coating of white
slip for appropriate decoration by fine painting of
funeral or memorial subjects in red outline, to which
brown, green and blue washes are sometimes added.
Drinking-cups on which the same technique has been
employed are amongst the most attractive of all
Athenian wares.

The "François Vase" mentioned above is signed
both by the potter Ergotimus who made it and the
painter Clitias who decorated it. It is thus an early
example of a practice which has persisted intermittently
down to the present day, that of painting or stamping
on pottery the name or mark of the firm that made it
and sometimes also that of the artist who decorated
it. Thanks to this habit, which was general at Athens
especially in the fifth century B.C., we can differentiate
the work of many Attic painters whose names are now
famous, but a discussion of their several styles lies
outside the scope of a general survey.

In the fifth century Athens was mistress of the
Greek seas and ousted Corinth as the chief trading
city; amongst the exports carried by Athenian ships
to all parts of the Mediterranean was the earthenware
which was one of the city's chief products. Hence it
comes that the first Greek vases known to archæologists were those found in the tombs of Tuscany; they

PLATE II

A. Dish, *sgraffiato* ware, Italian (Victoria and Albert Museum)
(*Page* 28)

B. "Red-figure" cup, Attic (Victoria and Albert Museum)
(*Page* 15)

were believed to be Etruscan, and the factory built by
Wedgwood for the manufacture of vases in imitation
of them was named by him " Etruria " (compare p. 45).
Not only the cities of Etruria but the Greek colonies in
the south of Italy were profitable customers of the
Athenian potters. The result has its parallel again and
again in later history; the craftsmen of the importing
cities were driven to competition by imitation of the
technique and style of the wares by which their local
trade was threatened. In Campania, Lucania and
Apulia vast quantities of " red-figure " vases were made
during the fourth century and onwards until the Greek
colonies were conquered by Rome. At first they resembled their rivals, but by degrees they developed
styles of their own; with their overcrowded figure-
subjects (very often illustrating scenes on the stage)
and their elaborate detail they show a rapid decline,
no less in technical than in artistic competence; in
the effort to make them more attractive, polychrome
painting in various earthy pigments was employed to
enliven the simple red and black. But no such ex-
pedients could make up for inferior quality, and it is
with small regret that we turn to the consideration of
new and less ambitious types by which they were
succeeded.

In the Hellenistic period (third and second centuries
B.C.) vase-painting passed through a last and not un-
attractive phase before it died away altogether in
competition with an easier manner of decorating
pottery. The " red-figure " technique disappeared,
and a new method was employed; light designs on a
dark ground were obtained by painting in opaque
white or buff over the black glaze. The subjects so
rendered, sometimes small figures but often no more
than simple wreaths of vine or ivy, have the undeniable
charm of prettiness which is the mark of Alexandrian
art in the last centuries of the pre-Christian era. It
was an age of luxury, in which pottery was employed

only for humbler uses and gold or silver with chased
embossments was the chosen material for the wine-
cup and flagon. For those who could not afford such
splendour the potters began to make wares moulded
in relief with designs copied from those of the goldsmith, whether figure-subjects or mere floral and conventional ornament; these earthenware substitutes are
of great interest to the archæologist because they give
evidence of the character of the vessels which have
paid the price of their costlier material by trans-
mutation in the melting-pot.

The technique of relief moulding thus developed by
Hellenistic potters was passed on by them to their
successors under the Roman Emperors. Pliny speaks
of a fine kind of earthenware known as " Samian ",
probably because it was originally made in the island
of Samos, as being produced at Arretium (Arezzo, in
Tuscany); the discovery of kiln-wasters at that place
has made it possible to identify this Arretine variety
of " Samian " with a fine red earthenware, moulded
with a large variety of figure-subjects in relief and
coated with a hard, very thin, bright red glaze; the
beauty and the accurate modelling of the naked
figures and draperies prove a high degree of accomplishment in the craftsmen who cut the moulds in which
the wares were pressed. " Samian " ware of the same
class but varying in quality was made in other widely
distant parts of the Roman Empire; a kiln has recently
been unearthed at Colchester, proving that not all the
" Samian " found in such quantities in Great Britain
(as indeed on most sites of Roman occupation) was
imported from Gaul, as has often been assumed. The
fact remains, however, that potteries in Gascony had a
vast overseas trade in the second and third centuries
after Christ, and they are shown by the potters' names
with which the wares are usually stamped to have
produced most of the " Samian " of good quality dug
up in England. Much of this ware is decorated in the

manner of the Arretine " Samian ", but very clumsily,
with figures and other reliefs (sometimes of archæological interest for the evidence they give, for instance, relating to circus games and gladiatorial con-
tests); far more pleasing, however, are the perfectly plain
bowls, cups and flat dishes made for ordinary domestic
use, equalling with their hard bright surface and
clean-cut profiles modern table china of good quality.
Amongst the centres that made good " Samian " ware
was Cologne, whence also it was exported to Britain;
the Cologne variety often has reliefs " trailed " on in
slip in the manner of Staffordshire slip ware of the
seventeenth century (compare p. 32). Another Staffordshire procedure found already in " Samian " ware and
invented apparently quite independently in China and
other parts of the world, is the mingling of clays of
different colours to produce a mottled " body " in
imitation of the markings of agate or marble. It may
be mentioned here that long before the period of the
fine Arretine ware Etruria had native plain red and
black wares of its own, uninfluenced by Greece, in
which the Roman liking for relief decoration was
anticipated; the most remarkable are the great oviform
jars in red earthenware of the seventh century B.C.
vertically fluted and decorated round the shoulder by
means of a wood block cut in intaglio, with reliefs of
animals or hunting-scenes repeated in oblong compartments (it is, however, possible that these, though
found in Etruscan tombs, were not indigenous).

When the Romans expanded their dominions beyond
the Alps they came into contact with a pre-existing Celtic
civilization, named after the locality in which the most
important evidences of it were found—La Tène, in
Switzerland, near Neuchâtel; this, in turn, had about
500 B.C. replaced a still earlier culture of high standard
(called for a similar reason after Hallstatt, in Upper
Austria) and its predecessor in the Bronze Age. The
rough Neolithic pottery already mentioned (p. 3) was

succeeded by better made wares in the Bronze Age,
such as the finely-shaped urns with high neck and
mammiform bosses found in Lusatia. The most remarkable pottery of the Hallstatt period is the ware
found in South West Germany—platters and bulbous
and oviform jars—with lozenges, zigzags and chequer
patterns painted, with an effect almost of gaiety, in
red and black earth pigments on the buff "body" (a
type which survived into the succeeding period). The
La Tène wares are the first produced north of the
Alps for making which the potter's wheel, doubtless
introduced from the south, was used. The types are
various. Great distinction of form is shown by grey
and black wares of fine "body", examples of which
have been dug up both in France and in England,
in shapes of elegant profile rising from a narrow base to
a high shoulder which is either rounded or, under the
influence of vessels in bronze, turned inward at a sharp
angle; in one class the sweep of the profile is broken
at well-judged intervals by groups of convex ribs.
The smooth burnished surface of these wares needed
no pattern to make it attractive and often has none;
occasionally a simple pattern has been scratched in the
clay, or pressed in with a blunt-pointed stick producing
a polished line, as, for instance, the repeated step-
motive on the shoulder of a beautiful jar, in the British
Museum, from Mesnil-les-Hurlus, in Champagne (fig. 3).
The most ambitious of these pre-Roman wares in Gaul
are certain urns painted in red on a darker ground
with the splendid "Celtic scroll" motive, which survived in Ireland to enrich the design of goldsmiths'
work and illuminated manuscripts in early Christian
times.

Pottery akin to these early Celtic wares continued
to be made by natives in Gaul and Britain, little influenced by contact with Classical art, during the
Roman occupation. In Britain various types have
been distinguished in addition to the red "Samian"

ware, both home-made and imported, which has been mentioned above (p. 18). Chief of these are the bur-

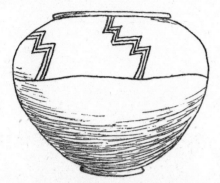

Fig. 3.—Gaulish jar (British Museum)

nished black wares made on the site of Upchurch, near Rochester, which perpetuate in a modest way the sleek, well-proportioned shapes of their Celtic fore-

Fig. 4.—Romano-British (Castor) cup (British Museum)

runners, and those found on a kiln-site at Castor, near Peterborough. The Castor wares, notably goblets with wide mouth and narrow base (fig. 4), display a delightful technique already mentioned (p. 19) which was occasionally used elsewhere in the Roman Empire (as at Cologne and in Egypt); this is the use of clay " slip ", sometimes white on a dark ground, sometimes of the same colour as the " body ", trailed on in high relief to form running scrollwork, almost " Gothic " in feeling, or, very cleverly, in vigorous if crude representations of chariot-races, combats or deer pursued by hounds. Another Castor type, also paralleled at Cologne, is a

Fig. 5.—Green-glazed Egypto-Roman cup (Fitzwilliam Museum, Cambridge)

jar with vertical indentations round the sides, sometimes with tiers of overlapping clay scales pressed on with the thumb on the intervening ridges left by the depressions. Such wares as these, unpretentious as they are, prove their makers to have been potters with a sure sense of the possibilities of their art.

In Egypt, the home of glass (see pp. 126–128), there was a highly important development when the Roman technique of relief moulding, which is the chief feature of " Samian ", was combined with a glaze containing lead. Recent research suggests that this innovation may have been the result of trade contacts with China (see p. 51). However this may be, in early Imperial times two-handled cups and other small vessels were being made, with charming reliefs of foliage and other

ornament derived from goldsmiths' work, under a rich
lead glaze, either yellow or stained with copper to a
deep green (fig. 5). Where this lead-glazed pottery was
made is uncertain, but it is likely to have been at
Alexandria.

An explanation may here be given in parenthesis
of the omission of any detailed account of ancient
American pottery. The early wares of Peru, often
modelled in the shape of men and animals, and the
no less remarkable Mexican wares painted in delightful
harmonies of black, red, buff and white either with very
elaborate pictorial subjects or with quasi-geometrical
designs of great dignity, have had no effect upon the
outside world until quite recent times (through the
channel of the related later American Indian wares).
The same is the case with the pottery of the black
races of Africa, which for its beauty of form would
otherwise be deserving of a place.

CHAPTER III

The European Tradition of Clay Technique

THE centuries that followed the fall of the Roman Empire were in Western Europe a period in which the arts generally were at a low ebb. Pottery was amongst those which, if not altogether extinguished, had a struggle for existence; the centre of civilization had shifted eastwards, and it was in the East alone, as we shall see, that pottery of any sort of refinement was being made during the Dark Ages, or even in the later mediæval period when other arts were flourishing in full brilliance. This is not to say that in the Middle Ages western lands did not produce wares of any æsthetic value. Visitors to archæological museums in the Rhineland, France, England and even Denmark will find mediæval wares full of vigorous character, compelling admiration by their formal qualities and the sense they prove in their makers of the essential possibilities of clay.

An important point here arises. If we compare an early Bronze Age pot such as that reproduced in fig. 1 with a piece of Chinese *famille verte* porcelain of the eighteenth century—such a thing, to name an example, as a good dish or vase of a familiar kind with a painting of a lady in a garden—it is likely that both will give us pleasure; but we are conscious that the stimulation is of an entirely different kind in the two cases. The Bronze Age pot moves us by its plastic quality; its goodness is that of a soft material kneaded and guided into shape by the pressure of hands. The Chinese dish or vase on the other hand makes its appeal almost entirely as graphic design, by the fine draughtsmanship of its decoration, enhanced by brilliant and harmonious colours; it has such impelling attractiveness of this order that it is hardly thought of as plastic art at all. The difference is a vital one between two classes of pottery and has been apparent already in the Greek vases discussed in the last chapter. In general it is true that, wherever suitable ceramic pigments have been available, and increasingly as their range widened in variety, potters have been tempted to neglect the opportunities for decorative enhancement offered by the qualities of their essential material; they have turned away rather to mediums of an entirely different order, namely, metallic pigments capable of withstanding heat and brought within their scope by enlisting the help of a fluxing agent which, whether described as glass, glaze or enamel, is in substance one and the same. Purists may say that in so doing they have been traitors to their art, but in their apostasy they have produced such loveliness of another kind that few will deny them forgiveness. The wares to be dealt with in this chapter are those in which the tradition of working in clay has been kept up, without recourse (or mainly so) to the ancillary art of the painter. To this group the wares of Western Europe in the main belong, and particularly those of England, where the tradition has been dominant till the verge of modern times. In countries such as China and Italy, where painting has been a leading, if not *the* leading art, and the technique of glazes and enamels has been better understood and mastered, polychrome painted pottery has more readily made itself at home.

Before more is said in detail of English pottery of the Middle Ages an explanation is needed of a feature that distinguishes it at once from the pottery made in

Britain in Roman times and from the rough wares,
similar to those made on the Continent, of the Anglo-
Saxon period. A lead glaze is almost always present,
as at least a partial covering of the surface. It seems
likely that the secret of its use was learnt by the English
potters from France, and it is virtually certain that
ultimately it was derived from the Levant. We have
seen (p. 22) that fine lead-glazed earthenware was
being made in the first centuries after Christ in Egypt
(probably at Alexandria) and in other parts of the
Roman Empire, including Italy. The use of such a
glaze doubtless endured without a break in the latter
country, as may be gathered for instance from the
pitchers with tubular spout dug up in the Forum at
Rome and attributed to the eighth and ninth centuries; they have a simple but effective decoration of
pads or scales of clay stuck on before glazing.[1] Very
similar pitchers have been found in Constantinople.

In this latter city, and elsewhere in the Levant—for
instance, in Cyprus, Syria and Palestine—potsherds
are dug up of lead-glazed earthenware with decoration
which, though differing in motives of design, shows
everywhere an identical technique[2]; this is effected by
covering the buff or red " body " with a surface-
coating of white clay slip through which, when it has
dried sufficiently, a design is scratched with a pointed
tool, or scraped away, so as to reveal the darker colour
underneath, the whole being subsequently protected
by a bath of transparent lead glaze, which may range
in colour from a pale cream to a deep amber yellow;

[1] Compare G. Ballardini, *La maiolica italiana dalle origini alla fine del Cinquecento*, Florence, 1938, fig. 1.

[2] Kiln-sites producing wares of the type in question have lately been located at the Crusaders' harbour, Port Saint Symeon, near Antioch, where they seem to have ceased operation when the place was captured by the Sultan of Egypt in 1268.

(See *Victoria and Albert Museum, Review of Principal Acquisitions during 1937*, pp. 17–8, fig. 1; Arthur Lane, " The Early Sgraffito Ware of the Near East ", pp. 51–4, in *Transactions of the Oriental Ceramic Society*, XV, 1937–8; *id.*, " Medieval finds at Al Mina in North Syria," pp. 45–53, in *Archæologia*, LXXXVII, 1938.)

it has long been the custom for convenience to apply to wares showing this technique the Italian term *sgraffiato* ("scratched"), which however, it should be stated, is not employed by Italian writers.[1] Where this technique originated is a problem still awaiting definite solution. Examples of it are not unknown in China, dating probably from the ninth century A.D.; it is common in Central Asia (as at Samarkand) in the same period. In Persia the technique was practised with superb artistic effect on wares attributed to the eleventh and twelfth centuries, although in that country it must have been a less costly substitute for painting in metallic lustre and other pigments (compare p. 63). The potsherds found on kiln-sites at Fostat (Old Cairo) prove that it had a similar status in Egypt. These Egyptian lead-glazed wares, which continued in currency as late as the fifteenth century and range from crude crockery to work of fine artistic quality, are of particular interest, because they show an understanding of the exploitation of pure clay technique in a wide variety of manners, always over a groundwork of coarse, deep red earthenware. The *sgraffiato* method is sometimes used without further elaboration, but very often, in rendering either the coats of arms of the Mameluke nobles, or birds, animals and plant forms, or zones of Arabic inscription, the scratched outlines are filled in with painting in thick clay pigment, white and red, sometimes in combination. Again, such "slip painting" is employed alone, in much the same manner as on the Staffordshire wares to be described later, whilst a further diversity may be given by staining the glaze—usually brown or straw-coloured—bright or olive green with copper. The Byzantine *sgraffiato* ware dug up at Constantinople, Athens, Salonica and elsewhere is also of interest with its frequent employment of Christian

---

[1] *Sgraffio* (either a noun, "a scratch", or a verb, "I scratch"—it is difficult to decide which is intended) occurs in Piccolpasso's account of this class of ware (compare p. 88, below), and from this word modern English writers seem to have adopted the participial *sgraffiato*.

emblems such as the dove and cross and of Greek
sacred monograms; it also rises occasionally to a level
of fine artistic quality.

It will be well here to speak of the *sgraffiato* ware
of Italy, where the technique was practised with more
splendid accomplishment than anywhere else. Employed doubtless on a humble scale in mediæval times,
it suddenly rose, in the region north of the Appenines
and under the influence of the dawning Renaissance,
to the production of true masterpieces of design; the
skilled draughtsmanship of the potters is shown not
only in their rendering of hares, lions, and other animals,
but, above all, in the delineation of the human figure,
often in complex and superbly balanced compositions.
The all-encompassing art of the great masters of painting
with which these potters, like all their fellow-citizens,
were in daily contact, unquestionably stimulated them
to such high attainment; the more immediate impulse
is to be found in the activities of their fellow-craftsmen
who possessed the secret of maiolica-painting (to be
described at length on a later page), and constituted a
formidable rival claim on the patronage of their clients.
Sgraffiato wares of almost indistinguishable character
were made in several places, but supremacy in this
branch of craftsmanship towards the end of the fifteenth century belongs to Padua and above all to
Bologna. Examples may be seen in the national collections. A dish in the Victoria and Albert Museum, with
elegant figures of a mandoline player in the company
of a lady and another youth (Plate II, A), represents a
type attributed to Padua, paralleled three centuries
earlier in a certain class of Persian *sgraffiato* ware; in
this the whole of the ground is scraped away, leaving
the figures silhouetted in slight relief, whilst touches of
blue, green, purple and amber-yellow pigment are
added to give diversity of colour. A great basin, also
at South Kensington, with three lions modelled in the
round to support it, and the subject of a naked man

wrestling with a dragon engraved inside it, represents the Bologna ware of about 1490, in which the touches of pigment are limited to green and brown; from the same workshop comes a dish in the British Museum with two figures in dress of the period accompanied by shields with emblems of the Visconti and Este families. This high standard was not long maintained, and in the seventeenth century Italian *sgraffiato* ware dropped to the level of a rather ragged peasant art.

From this survey of antecedents and collaterals we return to follow the story of English pottery of the native type. There is no evidence to show that pottery was made in England after the overthrow of the Romano-British civilization until the thirteenth or perhaps the twelfth century, and everything seems to indicate that the craft was reintroduced from abroad after the Norman Conquest. It is likely that thereafter pottery kilns were set up to supply local needs in any part of the country where suitable clay was at hand, and remains of mediæval kilns, or kiln " wasters ", have been found amongst other places at Nottingham, Lincoln, Ely, Hastings, Rye, Cheam, Barnstaple, and near Hereford, whilst groups of pots dug up in various localities showing characteristics in common and differing from those of other groups, justify the presumption of workshops once existing in or near London, York, Bristol, Salisbury, and Oxford. Amongst the earliest types two, occurring in London finds, are conspicuous, a graceful spindle-shaped jug, wide-spreading at the base, with an excellent glaze stained dark green with copper; and a high pitcher, generally showing only a smear of glaze and peculiar for the convexity of the neck, repeating that of the body and drawn in bluntly to a flangeless mouth. Jugs from the Cheam kiln are remarkable for bold scroll foliage painted in dark brown, indicating by its style a date little if at all after 1300. In the fourteenth century the tendency is towards broader proportions, with stout capacious body and handle firmly pressed on, trefoil-like depressions being scooped out with the thumb at its base (the thoroughly satisfactory attachment of the handle is an almost invariable feature of these mediæval jugs, in marked contrast with many of more recent make). Glazes vary in colour from yellow and brown to greyish or bright green, and decoration of some kind becomes general. Sometimes this consists of a few lines scratched with a stick, but very often the plastic quality of clay has been used to advantage in adding ornament in slight relief (Plate III, A). A few only of the many varieties of relief decoration can be named—studs like those on the jugs found in Rome (see p. 26); small shreds of clay stuck on either in vertical stripes—exactly as on some mediæval jugs from Constantinople in the Kaiser Friedrich Museum, Berlin—or covering the whole surface with a scale-pattern (the latter especially on examples found in London); on several pots found at Oxford, bold Gothic scroll-work in narrow strips of clay with small indentations giving the aspect of a coiled chain; somewhat ungainly bearded masks and arms with elbows akimbo seem to be a feature employed especially at Cambridge and elsewhere in the East; York shows in its museum a noble array of squat brownish-green jugs with applied reliefs such as heraldic shields and devices or ears of corn, shaped in moulds probably of wood. An early jug with a shield on the front, in the Royal Museum, Canterbury, proves that the *sgraffiato* technique (compare p. 27) was not unknown. To the fourteenth century or perhaps earlier belong the vessels of animal form—one such represents a mounted knight in armour—of which examples can be seen in several museums; their inspiration was derived from the well-known ewer in bronze or silver known as an aquamanile and used in washing the hands, and it is interesting to note that the idea had been adopted some four centuries earlier, as may be seen from a specimen in the museum at

PLATE III

A. Earthenware pitcher, English,
   fourteenth century *(Page 30)*

B. Stoneware jug, Westerwald
    (Page 37)

C. Stoneware jug made by Dwight
   (Page 39)

D. Slipware mug, Staffordshire
    (Page 33)

(A London Museum: B, C, D, Fitzwilliam Museum, Cambridge)

Spires, by a Carolingian potter of the Rhineland closely copying a bronze original from Syria or Persia.

In the fifteenth century London seems to have taken the lead in the direction of polychrome decoration by employing for such relief ornaments clays (sometimes more than one) differing in colour from that of the pot itself, perhaps further helped out with touches of copper-green; thus it was possible to produce so gay an object as a jug in the London Museum, with red flowers on green stalks in relief on a primrose-yellow ground, or another very handsome one, at Maidstone, with a bold chevron pattern in brown set with a row of studs in buff. Jugs have been dug up at Copenhagen so similar in technique and appearance as to indicate some sort of contact between English and Danish potters at this time. In the Tudor period there seems to have been a reversion to simpler types, as shown in some neatly shaped jugs with a good bright green glaze and in the red wares—particularly inverted conical or bell-shaped cups with three or four handles—fired to the hardness of stoneware and covered with a thick sheeny dark brown glaze. The latter, from being found in numbers on the sites of monasteries of the Order, are commonly classed as " Cistercian ware "; they were certainly being made before the Dissolution, and are the forerunners of the Staffordshire brown-glazed wares of the seventeenth century. An exception to such plainness is afforded by green- or yellow-glazed stove-tiles, candle-sconces and flasks moulded with the Royal Arms and emblems in relief, which seem to have been made in a London workshop, probably by an immigrant from Germany, one of the many foreign craftsmen employed for the Court of Henry VIII.

In the seventeenth century native English pottery assumed the character of " slip ware " in its manifold varieties, and this continued as a form of peasant art in out-of-the-way places well into the nineteenth

century. Its characteristic is the decoration effected
by the manipulation of clay, either white or buff,
red, dark brown or greenish-grey,[1] mixed with water to
a creamy consistency (compare p. 22). This " slip "
may be used to carry out inscriptions or representational designs, by trailing it on out of a spout in the
manner of sugar icing on a cake, or it may be applied
in pads and then stamped with a pattern in relief, or
it may be laid on in bands of two or more colours and
then, with a wire brush, worked into markings like
those of a stone or combed into regular feather-patterns,
often of great beauty. Very occasionally in England
the *sgraffiato* technique was used; clays of different
colours were also mingled not merely superficially but,
as long before by the Ancient Romans and the Chinese,
to make the " agate ware " out of which a pot was
thrown or moulded.

The earliest of the English slip wares are those
made in or near London, with inscriptions often of a
Puritanical turn (" Watch and pray," " Be not hy
minded "), in white on red, and at Wrotham, in Kent;
the latter place is known especially for nearly cylindrical
drinking-pots known as " tygs ", with stamped or
trailed reliefs and four handles, each double-looped,
generally with a plait of red and white clay neatly
embedded in a groove cut down the upper loop. Yorkshire, Somerset and Devon had their slip ware potteries
with their own local peculiarities lasting till the middle
of the nineteenth century; workshops in the Weald
of Sussex and Kent developed a kind, very attractive
at its best, in which artless designs were impressed in
the red ware with small stamps or printers' types
and then inlaid with white clay—a technique analogous
to that of the splendid English floor-tiles of the Middle
Ages. Amongst all these centres of a rustic craft the
neighbourhood of Burslem in North Staffordshire soon

---

[1] It must be understood that these colours are those assumed by the clay
after firing, not of the clay in its raw condition.

began to take the lead owing to certain advantages of situation; amongst these were coal at their very doors instead of wood for firing their kilns, as well as suitable beds of clay, and good facilities for the distribution of their wares by water, enabling the Staffordshire potters to outstrip their competitors and to start on a career which was to bring their successors to the very forefront of the ceramic industry of the world.

The Staffordshire slip wares show such diversity that anything like a complete survey of them would here be out of place. Mention may be made in particular of the great, highly decorative dishes which, side by side with the simpler combed or marbled dishes made for ordinary use in the kitchen or bakehouse, were turned out late in the seventeenth and early in the eighteenth century presumably to celebrate special occasions such as weddings or birthdays. They display sometimes rude but vigorous figures or busts of the king and queen, sometimes shields or heraldic animals, lions, eagles, mermaids, and so forth, or merely conventional tulips, roses or other flowers, trailed on in dark lines, afterwards as a rule dotted with white, the figures being filled in with flat washes of contrasting colour. A name inscribed on the rim is a very common accompaniment, and most of the finest examples of this type of dish bear that of Thomas Toft; whether he was their maker or their recipient is a question still undecided, but the balance of opinion is in favour of the former interpretation. Dishes are not the only articles decorated in this manner and similarly inscribed; covered posset-pots with a sucking-spout for serving hot drinks, jugs, mugs, models of cradles for keepsakes (or perhaps pipe-trays) also occur, and it is on some of these that the delightful combed feather-ornament is seen in a perfection which entitles such articles to a high place in the realm of ceramic achievement (Plate III, D).

Hitherto we have seen the English potters in their

country workshops pursuing their local and highly individual craft on traditional lines quite undisturbed by influence from the outside world. In the reign of Charles II, however, something happened which brought with it the seeds of revolution. The Dutch and English East India merchants had, since the beginning of the century, been bringing to western Europe not only silk and lacquer but also, for the first time as a regular article of import, Chinese porcelain, and to this list was now added tea. Tea-drinking at once became the fashion, and to meet it suitable teapots and cups began also to be brought from the East. Through the enterprise, at first, of two Dutch silversmiths, brothers named Elers, who came to England with William of Orange, efforts were made to compete with these imported tea-table wares by home production, and the Staffordshire potters saw established in their immediate neighbourhood a workshop for making hard red ware superficially much like the Chinese. The consequence was a speedy reform in the traditional methods of the district in the direction of refined workmanship.

But at the same time other extraneous influences were beginning to operate, and for the understanding of these a long digression is necessary. Pottery during the Middle Ages in Germany did not for the most part fall into the class of lead-glazed earthenware. The museums of Mainz and other cities in the Rhineland show us mediæval wares admirable in shape and often with striking geometrical and other formal decorations, either incised and impressed or painted in dark earth pigments, but generally destitute of glaze. One of the advantages given by glaze was obtained by firing the wares to a high temperature so that they became hard and impervious, and thus stoneware, already known to China, was evolved quite independently in Europe. Stoneware is perhaps the outstanding German contribution to the process of ceramic evolution. In the region of Mainz are found jars, sometimes with lids, and jugs, attributed to the fourteenth and fifteenth centuries, made of a hard unglazed ware either grey or dark red with a tendency to a chocolate tone; they are mostly without decoration, but their strong horizontal ribs give them a great attractiveness to those who like to see in a pot some traces of its creation on the wheel. Dreihausen, near Marburg, in Hesse, was a place in which dark red stoneware of this kind continued to be made for centuries; some of the more showy pieces of this Dreihausen ware, in its earlier period, were carved before firing with very elaborate deep-cut ornament like the traceries of the late Gothic windows of the time.

It was, however, lower down the Rhine valley that the great German stoneware industry was to find its lasting home. At Siegburg, near Bonn, a pale cream-coloured stoneware was made from about 1300 until the city was sacked by a Swedish army in 1632 and its potters sought refuge elsewhere. The principal earlier productions were tall slender jugs with pronounced horizontal ridges, which were widely exported throughout the north and to England. In the sixteenth century Siegburg adopted the mode of decoration which was common amongst the stoneware-potters of the Rhineland; reliefs made by pressing in moulds of baked clay or soft stone were stuck on to suitable parts of the surface, accessory ornament being added either by incising with a pointed tool or by repeated impressions with small brass stamps. The most characteristic of the standard Siegburg shapes is a tall tankard (called *Schnelle*) with sides tapering slightly upwards; it lent itself to the application of three vertical strips or pads on which would be reliefs either of single standing figures, or of medallions in tiers with floral or scroll ornament between. For the subjects of these reliefs the mould-cutters drew on the engravings of the German " Little Masters " of the period, whose repertory covered not only Biblical scenes and emblematic figures but also a few themes from classical mythology. Shields of arms and occasionally portraits of contemporary sovereigns also occur. One of the finest examples of Siegburg stoneware in existence is the centrepiece in the form of a wine-cistern and candlestick combined made for the potters' guild and decorated with the arms of the Empire and of the neighbouring duchy of Juliers, Cleves and Berg; it is in the Victoria and Albert Museum.

The earlier Siegburg and other stonewares were un-glazed and, as stoneware is non-porous, glazing is of less importance than on earthenware, but in the six-teenth century and later it was customary to glaze stoneware also. This is done by shovelling common salt through holes into the kiln when a high degree of temperature has been reached; the salt vaporizes, the chlorine in it combining with the carbon from the fuel as hydrochloric acid gas, whilst the sodium unites with the silica and alumina of the clay to form what is known as a salt glaze on the surface of the wares. If the clay has a large iron content or if a ferruginous surface-dressing has been applied to the wares before firing, this glaze takes on a deep brown colour.

Cologne had several stoneware kilns, until about 1570, when owing to the danger of fire in the city their owners removed to the neighbouring town of Frechen. The wares of both places are distinguished by their rich brown glaze, which in later wares of Frechen tends to coagulate in thick blotches. The relief decoration is similar in technique to that of Siegburg but as a rule simpler, being often confined, on jugs, to a band round the waist and one or two small medallions with busts or rosettes; but a common feature, begun at Cologne and continued especially at Frechen, is a bearded man's mask applied on the front of the neck. In the seventeenth century vast numbers of fat-bellied Frechen jugs of this kind, often very crudely made, found their way across the sea for use in England, perhaps filled with Rhenish wine, and were given the name of " grey-beards " or " Bellarmines ", in uncomplimentary allu-sion to the cardinal of that name, unpopular in Pro-testant countries. The consequences of this export trade will be related after the remaining classes of German stoneware have been briefly reviewed.

The other chief centre of the stoneware industry in the 16th century was at Raeren, near Aix-la-Chapelle. The earlier Raeren wares have a rich brown glaze and are conspicuous for their admirable shapes, sometimes of large proportions, which show in their makers a fine, almost architectural sense of form; in technique —applied reliefs and stamping—and in the content of the motives of decoration employed they are not different from the wares of Cologne and Siegburg. Towards the end of the century the greatest of the Raeren master-potters, Jan Emens, introduced a new class of stoneware made of a clay burning to a light bluish grey, at the same time using cobalt-blue pigment applied before firing, to colour the background of the reliefs and in other details. After 1600 the Raeren potteries declined and the industry shifted to Grenz-hausen, Höhr and other villages in the Westerwald district, near Coblenz. Here at first the traditions of the Raeren blue-and-grey ware were followed. Later in the century a different style was developed; a rich manganese purple was pleasantly and effectively com-bined with the blue for ground colouring, and incised ornament played an increasing part as an auxiliary to the moulded reliefs. Typical of this stage are the large jugs with cylindrical neck, generally reeded, and globular body showing on the front a shield or mono-gram in relief flanked by formal flowers or palmettes, also moulded, with stems in the form of wavy bands incised in the clay; such jugs were largely made for export abroad and are often found in England with the portraits of William and Mary or crowned cipher of Queen Anne or George I (Plate III, B). The Wester-

wald continued till modern times to produce stoneware, but of inferior quality.

The only important manufacture of stoneware in
Germany elsewhere than in the Rhineland was at
Kreussen, in North Bavaria. Its characteristic products
in the seventeenth century were squat broad-based
tankards with reliefs picked out with somewhat garish
enamel colours and gilding fixed by a second, low-
temperature firing; the motives of decoration were to
a large extent those employed by the glass-enamellers
of the same region, and it is possible that the same
workshops enamelled both stoneware and glass (compare p. 147).

The large importations of Rhenish stoneware into
England prompted men of enterprise to introduce
the manufacture itself. Already in Queen Elizabeth's
reign a move was made in this direction, but there is
no certainty that stoneware was made in England
before 1626; in that year Charles I granted a patent
to Thomas Rous and Abraham Cullyn (alias Cullen),
one Dutch born, the other of Dutch extraction, for
making " stone " pots and bottles. Their kilns were
in London, at St. Andrew Undershaft. None of their
wares can be identified with certainty, but it is likely
that they resembled those imported from Frechen so
closely as to be almost indistinguishable from them.
A good case has been made out for the English origin
of a stoneware wine-jug, without the bearded mask of
the Frechen jugs (see p. 36), made about 1655 for the
landlord of the famous Cock Tavern in Fleet Street,
and a " greybeard " (dated 1660—that is, after both
Rous and Cullen were dead), both in the Ashmolean
Museum, Oxford.[1] With the year 1671 we come to the
activities as a potter of John Dwight, of Oxford, and
all uncertainties cease as to the nature of the stoneware made in England.

---

[1] See Aubrey J. Toppin, " Rous and Cullen, merchants and potters ", in
Transactions of the English Ceramic Circle, No. 5, 1937, pp. 38–48.

Dwight was in close touch with the circle of scientists who after the Restoration founded the Royal Society. In 1671 he took out a patent for the " Mistery of Transparent Earthenware commonly knowne by the Names of Porcelaine or China ", and " stone ware vulgarly called Cologne ware ", and three years later he was at Fulham, where he set up the stoneware pottery still in existence. Numerous specimens of ware have survived which can be attributed with certainty to Dwight. They include some rather crude " greybeards " in imitation of those made at Frechen, as well as bottles, a punchbowl and mugs not only in brown and marbled grey stoneware quite different from the German types (usually with small relief ornaments, amongst them busts of William and Mary, stamped on applied pads, Plate III, c), but also in a fine white stoneware which, where it is thin, is translucent like porcelain; this white ware was the outcome of an innovation of Dwight's which was later to have important consequences, in Staffordshire—the mixture with the clay of flints calcined and ground to a powder. Fragments of a Westerwald blue-and-purple jug (compare p. 37) discovered at the Fulham pottery with other evidences of his work explain the reference by his friend Dr. Plot to his discovery of " the mystery of the Hessian wares ". It is almost certain also that some of the mugs and cups imitating the imported Chinese red stoneware (compare p. 34) are from Dwight's kilns. Their most remarkable productions, however, were a number of busts and statuettes modelled in white or in bronze-coloured stoneware, masterpieces by a hand as yet unidentified, including a life-size portrait of Prince Rupert and a series of classical gods and heroes. After Dwight's death this high standard was not maintained, and the output of the Fulham pottery consisted chiefly of jars and tankards for use in taverns —sturdy wares decorated with applied reliefs of hunting-scenes, inn-signs, busts of the reigning sovereign and other subjects. Precisely similar articles were made also in stoneware potteries at Lambeth, which have continued in operation to the present day.

From London the manufacture had spread before 1700 to the Midlands. Nottingham made very attractive stoneware of admirable form with a lustrous brown glaze and decoration of several kinds including freely incised sprays of flowers and scrollwork. The earlier Staffordshire stoneware has only lately been identified, partly with the help of brown-glazed wasters with relief portraits of Queen Anne dug up a few years ago at Burslem.[1]

This sketch of the history of stoneware in Europe has been necessary in order to explain how, at the end of the seventeenth century, the Staffordshire potters were brought indirectly under stimulating influences from China and Germany, the first through the settlement in their neighbourhood of the Dutch brothers Elers, the second through competition with the manufacture of salt-glazed stoneware, lately introduced into England; important also was their learning the secret discovered by John Dwight, that a white-bodied ware could be made by adding burnt flints to the " body ", for only with wares not only dainty in shape but also light in colour could they hope to compete with the novel attractions of snow-white Chinese porcelain. Two potters named Twyford and Astbury are credited with some of the improvements which were speedily effected in the quality of the Staffordshire wares.

An early refinement was the addition, to the unglazed red ware with small stamped ornaments of the kind made by Dwight and the Elers brothers, of the traditional lead glaze, giving it a glossy surface of deep red tone; interesting diversity was obtained by using dabs of white pipe-clay instead of the red clay for the little stamped reliefs, and the same form of decoration

---

[1] See W. B. Honey, "English salt-glazed stoneware", in *Transactions of the English Ceramic Circle*, No. 1, 1933, p. 15.

was employed for wares made in clays firing to buff or dark brown. Teapots and jugs of coloured clay were sometimes given spouts and handles in white. The first step towards a white surface was the coating of the coloured body with a surface wash of fine white clay obtained from Devonshire; but the decisive move forward came when the Staffordshire men learned what, as we have seen, Dwight had found out before them, that a pure white " body " could be obtained by mixing flint with the lighter, yellow-firing plastic clays.

From now on for some time two different types of ware were being made by the Staffordshire potters out of the same "body" and in the same workshops. One of these was a white stoneware made by firing up to the heat necessary for fusion of the clay particles and glazing with salt—the famous Staffordshire " salt-glaze ware " (Plate IV, A); the date 1724 on specimens in the British and Fitzwilliam (Cambridge) Museums is the earliest recorded on this class of ware. The other type was earthenware fired at a lower temperature and covered with a lead glaze, a glaze which owing to the presence of iron impurities, continued to be of a yellowish straw or cream colour; this defect (as it appeared to the devotees of Chinese porcelain) was eliminated by later improvements. Identical decorations are found on both the salt- and the lead-glazed wares. On the earlier we have the familiar little stamped reliefs, sometimes ingeniously used by repetition and combination to build up pictorial subjects, as on the mugs and bowls made to celebrate Admiral Vernon's victory in the West Indies in 1739. In course of time, however, it was realized that relief decoration could be obtained much more easily by the use of moulds with the designs in intaglio. These were either of brass, alabaster or hard-fired clay, into which a slab or " bat " of clay (rolled out like pastry under a rolling-pin) could be pressed, the two halves of hollow vessels such as jugs or teapots being subsequently " luted " together at the edges; or else intaglio moulds of plaster were made in two halves from a block with ornament in relief and into these two halves, firmly lashed together, liquid slip was poured; the porous plaster drinking up the water leaves on the inside of the mould, after the superfluous liquid has been emptied out, a cast in clay which, when left to dry, can be released from the mould and is the pot, ready to go to the kiln for firing. This last is the casting process which has been in use in England since the middle of the eighteenth century for the manufacture of cheaper kinds of pottery.

One or two methods of decoration peculiar (in stone-ware) to Staffordshire salt-glaze call for mention; one of these is " scratch blue ", common about 1745–60, the scratching of floral designs or inscriptions in the soft clay and rubbing into it clay stained blue with cobalt (at an earlier stage similar " inlaid " designs had been done with dark brown clay). The other is painting in brilliant enamel colours fixed at a second firing, in emulation of painted porcelain, a practice which seems to have been introduced into Staffordshire by immigrant Dutch enamellers. Salt-glaze ware, attractive as it is in many ways, has disadvantages in use which cause it to go under in competition with the improved lead-glazed wares which must now be discussed.

One of the most enterprising Staffordshire potters about the middle of the century was Thomas Whieldon, of Fenton Low. He seems to have taken the lead in making the lead-glazed earthenware more attractive by diversity of colouring. Already in the early years of the century we find a glaze of a rich speckled purplish brown colour (derived from manganese) covering a buff " body " of the kind commonly used for the slip ware of the period. Whieldon used the same sort of glaze on wares made of the improved whitish body, and also a mottled effect—slate-blue, mouse-grey, bright green, and amber-yellow, as well as purple—obtained by

PLATE IV

A. Salt-glaze ware teapot, Staffordshire
(Page 41)

(All, Victoria and Albert Museum)

C. Chestnut-bowl, cream-coloured ware, Leeds
(Page 46)

B. Whieldon ware tureen, Staffordshire
(Page 43)

dabbing powdered ores to produce these colours on the surface before dipping in the bath of glaze (the process by now adopted instead of applying the glaze in a dry powdered state); this polychrome ware he called " tortoiseshell ". He decorated it either with moulded or cast reliefs, or by the process called " sprigging ", that is, by sticking on the surface leaves previously shaped in separate moulds and coiled stems made by rolling out cords of clay between the palms of the hands (Plate IV, B). Whieldon also made " agate wares ", of mingled clays differing in colour or stained blue with cobalt, of much greater refinement than his predecessors. Like other potters in Staffordshire he included amongst his output " black ware ", that is earthenware with a lead glaze stained to a glossy brownish black; it was made also at Jackfield in Shropshire, and has continued in favour for teapots to the present day.

In 1754 Whieldon took into partnership a man born twenty-four years before, at Burslem, of a family of potters, himself to be the forefather of distinguished descendants. This was Josiah Wedgwood, who in 1759 set up in his native place as a manufacturer on his own account. Wedgwood had the advantage not only of a thorough training in the craft of potting but also of an enterprising and inquiring temperament combined with æsthetic good taste, qualities which fitted him for the improvements he was to make in the local industry. Whilst in partnership with Whieldon he seems to have been responsible for the introduction of the rich copper-green glaze seen on tea-table wares moulded in the form of cauliflowers or pineapples. Possessed of a factory of his own, he made it his first purpose to improve the light-bodied " cream ware " of the district so as to accord better with rising standards of comfort and culture. He soon brought it to such perfection that he secured the patronage of Queen Charlotte and the right to name it " Queen's

ware " (Plate V, A). When, shortly after, the ingredients
of true porcelain—china clay and china stone—newly
discovered in Cornwall, were exploited with success in
the west of England (compare p. 110), Wedgwood was
one of the Staffordshire potters who took advantage
of the discovery by adding these materials to the ingredients of their earthenware. His good judgment
was seen also in the new shapes he adopted in conformity with the latest fashions of the day. These
were derived from the study of the antiquities of
Herculaneum and Pompeii, and of the vases found in
Etruscan tombs, then lately brought to the knowledge
of the cultured world by the publications of the Comte
de Caylus and of Sir William Hamilton, the British
Ambassador at Naples; it is interesting to note that
a copy of the great work on Sir William Hamilton's
collection was acquired by Wedgwood in 1769. Some
of his shapes show in their elegance that he was familiar
also with the contemporary silversmiths' work of
Birmingham and Sheffield.

Much of the Queen's ware was quite plain or decorated only with reliefs or openwork in the manner of
plate. Where painting was required it was carried out
in the local workshops which did the enamelling on
salt-glaze ware (compare p. 42); at a later period the
wares were sent from Burslem to be decorated at the
workshop in London, presently to be mentioned.
Transfer-printing over the glaze was also at this time
a popular method of decorating earthenware and
porcelain, and for this Wedgwood sent much of his
Queen's ware to the workshop of Sadler and Green
at Liverpool (compare p. 98).

In 1768 Wedgwood took into partnership his friend
Thomas Bentley, a Liverpool merchant of liberal
tastes who was keenly interested in the antique, and
they established the factory still existing near Hanley;
the first firing in it took place in the following year.
This new factory was intended at first entirely for the

production of ornamental wares (the " useful " Queen's
ware was to be made as before at Burslem, and so
continued till 1773, when the old factory was given
up), and the nature of these was indicated by the name
"Etruria" given to the works.   The first articles fired
were, in shape and partly in decoration, copies of an
ancient Greek " red-figure " vase. They were followed
by many literal but lifeless copies of the same kind,
from specimens borrowed for the purpose; the painting
on them was done not at Etruria but in the enamelling
workshop which had lately been established under
Bentley's supervision, first at their showrooms in
London and later at Chelsea, where enamellers who
had worked at the neighbouring porcelain factory were
available.   For these plagiarisms of the antique,
Wedgwood employed a new type of unglazed black
stoneware he had developed which he named " Egyptian
black " or " black basaltes ". By refining the local
red-firing and buff-firing clays he evolved new stone-
wares called " rosso antico " and " cane ware "; the
latter, as a concession to the fashion for *chinoiserie*
which persisted alongside the new neo-classical, as
may be seen in some of the furniture designs of Chip-
pendale, was often moulded and enamel-painted to
simulate bundles of bamboo. Proudest of all his
achievements in his own estimation was his " jasper
ware ", a fine stoneware containing barium in its composition, which could be stained blue, lilac, sage-green or
black and was generally decorated by the " sprigging "
process with moulded reliefs in white, including figure-
subjects imitating (in appearance but not in technique)
antique cameos (Plate XII, B). Like the black basaltes,
jasper, especially the favourite blue, was used not
only for vases and useful wares but also for making
all kinds of trinkets, as well as medallions with cameo
or intaglio figure-subjects after the antique and portrait busts; many of the latter representing persons
of the time are as excellent technically as they are

interesting. Most of these varieties of ware continue
to be made at Etruria to the present day, and they are
too familiar to need further description; what they
may lack in spontaneity of conception is partly made
good, in the earlier examples, by their high standard of
workmanship. Wedgwood's most famous performance
in this direction consisted in reproducing, in black
jasper, the ancient Roman cameo-cut glass vase known
as the " Portland Vase " (compare p. 132).

Vases in classical style were also made at Etruria
in glazed earthenware in imitation of agate, porphyry
and other such stones by improving upon the methods
employed by some of Wedgwood's predecessors. The
table services in Queen's ware were brought up to a
high level of refinement, being generally painted in
admirable taste with simple borders of vine, palmettes
and other classical motives in sober and harmonious
enamel colours. Wedgwood showed his good judgment
by engaging to work for him John Flaxman and other
competent artists. His great merit consists not so
much in inventing new types of ware for ornamental
vases as in organizing on a commercial basis the manufacture of " useful " ware of high quality, serviceable,
hygienic and at the same time æsthetically satisfying.

Wedgwood's success called forth a host of competitors,
some of whom were little behind him in the quality
of the goods they made. In his own district we find
amongst others Adams, Palmer, Turner, and Neale,
some of whom began their career as his assistants.
Outside Staffordshire his chief imitators were the
firm that brought up-to-date an old pottery at Leeds;
here and at one or two other factories in Yorkshire
excellent cream-coloured earthenware was made, the
Leeds ware being remarkable for its pierced decorations
done with great skill by hand-punching with small
metal stamps (Plate IV, c). Mention may here be made
also of the factory at Burslem owned by the Wood
family, in which towards the end of the eighteenth

PLATE V

A. Butter-box, Wedgwood's " Queen's ware " (Mrs. L. G. Drummond)
(Page 44)

B. Porcelain teapot, Worcester (Victoria and Albert Museum)
(Page 112)

centure the traditional colour-glaze painting technique
of their predecessors was continued in the output of
attractive wares, including a variety of figures, intended
for a humbler class of buyers than the fashionable
patrons of Wedgwood.

The cream-coloured ware of Wedgwood and his
imitators had such obvious advantages in use that it
killed the manufacture of delft ware (to be dealt with
later) and quickly became a serious rival even to
porcelain. Exported to the Continent and America, it
was so eagerly welcomed that foreign potters were
compelled to compete with it by themselves manu-
facturing the same kind of goods, often in slavish
imitation. Nothing contributed so much as this invasion from England to the decline of the time-honoured
maiolica and faïence which had flourished during the
eighteenth century in almost every country of Europe.

To complete the survey of the traditional technique
in Western Europe a few words must be added as to
its development on the Continent. French mediæval
lead-glazed pottery was similar in general character to
that of England but hardly its equal in originality
and vigour (conditions were perhaps less favourable
owing to a more widespread use in France of vessels
in other materials). It had, however, two remarkable
outgrowths in the Renaissance period. One of these,
flashing across the firmament of ceramic history like
a meteor and disappearing without leaving a trace of
influence behind it, is " Henri Deux ware ", first
appearing about 1525 but made chiefly in the reign of
that monarch—it would seem, in some small private
workshop at Saint-Porchaire, in Poitou. It was a soft
whitish earthenware with decoration in which applied
moulded reliefs were combined with openwork and
rows of small repeated ornaments impressed with book-
binders' stamps and inlaid with dark or light brown
clay. The designs are sometimes enlivened with touches
of green and blue painted on before the wares were

dipped in the pale cream-coloured lead glaze; in style they are highly sophisticated, reflecting the latest architectural fashions of the time, when flamboyant Gothic was yielding to the classical themes of the early Renaissance.

More lasting in their effect were the innovations of the famous Bernard Palissy, a glass-painter of Saintes, who took to making pottery. He tells us in his memoirs that he was inspired to do so by the sight of an earthenware cup, which was in all likelihood an example of the " Henri II ware " then being made in the same region as his home. His noteworthy achievement consisted in the development of lead glazes richly stained by mixing them with colouring oxides—blue, green, purple and amber-yellow—and in the employment of them as pigments on decoration moulded in relief. His earliest compositions were of a curious kind—casts made from snakes, crayfishes, beetles, ferns and other living creatures and plants of the local swamps and meadows, stuck in full relief on the surface of a dish in arrangements which display a genuine gift for design; later he adopted figure-subjects pressed in moulds after originals in brass or pewter, or formal designs in the fashion of the time made up of strapwork, rosettes, masks and foliage. Palissy won the royal patronage of Catherine de Médicis and was summoned to Paris, where he did some architectural work in colour-glazed earthenware for the queen, but he died a prisoner in the Bastille for his Protestant faith, in 1590. His sons and others carried on his work in potteries near Fontainebleau, but in steadily declining quality. Analogous wares with relief decoration in colours, in which, however, the glazes were mostly in the nature of enamels made opaque by using oxide of tin in their composition, were produced in the sixteenth century in several parts of Germany; some of the best, such as a great jug in the Victoria and Albert Museum with reliefs of the Adoration of the

Magi and the Massacre of the Innocents, come from the workshop of Paul Preuning at Nuremberg, but wares of a similar kind were made at Salzburg, Annaberg in Saxony, and perhaps elsewhere. At Neisse, in Silesia, a peculiar technique was adopted; a design was incised in outline with a sharp-pointed tool and then filled in with flat washes of coloured enamels of the same kind as those laid over the reliefs on the wares of Preuning and his followers.

The lead-glazing technique was not able to maintain itself on the Continent as it did in England. Confronted with the invasion of tin-enamelling and of porcelain from the East which will be related in another chapter, in France as in Germany and Switzerland, it was driven into the fastnesses of peasant art, the output of which, by no means always devoid of æsthetic merit, may be studied in such collections as that in the Fitzwilliam Museum, Cambridge. It returned, in an " improved " industrial form, routing its rivals, towards the end of the eighteenth century when, as we have seen, Wedgwood and his followers flooded European markets with their wares, compelling foreign manufacturers in self-defence to equip their own establishments for making *faïence fine* and *englisches Steingut*.

CHAPTER IV

China : The Invention of Porcelain

THE Chinese have proved themselves the greatest masters of the potter's art. Their porcelain has been a contribution to general culture with which their influence has penetrated throughout the world. Two causes may be named as having given them this advantage. In a contiguous region of the world—the East Indian archipelago—their neighbours were peoples so little civilized that they were able to make pottery either not at all or so frail and undurable that, as soon as navigation had brought them within reach of the mainland, they provided a ready market for the distribution of the thoroughly efficient Chinese goods. The second cause was the almost supernatural attractiveness of the white porcelain in itself, especially when enhanced with decoration in blue, which caused it to be welcome, like Chinese silk, even in the homes of ancient civilizations which had themselves been producing good pottery for thousands of years.

" Blue-and-white " is the most familiar and the most ubiquitous kind of Chinese porcelain, but it has no very long history; the lovely cobalt pigment was known in the West before it was introduced into China. It was with other classes of ware that the Chinese potters first spread their trade into the Western world.

About fifteen years ago exploration in the far Western Chinese province of Kansu disclosed the existence of a splendid type of earthenware made without the help of a wheel and attributable to the third millennium before Christ. It consists chiefly of large burial urns, usually more or less of inverted onion shape with two small loops projecting at the widest point, of buff ware painted in dark red, black and purplish brown with rhythmical swirling wave-motives of magnificent vitality, or leaf designs in reserve on a dark ground. There is no evidence, however, that the wonderful art displayed in these prehistoric urns had any long continuity. Pottery ceased to be important in China, and in the earlier dynastic periods bronze was the mistress art of the country, to such a degree that the unglazed earthenware vessels that have been found in tombs of these ages obviously follow in form bronze originals.

At some unknown date, perhaps as early as the third century but certainly many centuries after glass and glazing were known in Egypt, the Chinese also began to use glaze on their pottery. Tombs of the Han dynasty have yielded large quantities of a type of hard red ware generally with ornament moulded in relief and stuck on to the surface before the application of a glaze, which is either brown or stained deep green with copper; they include not only vessels " thrown " on the wheel (as a rule influenced in shape by bronze) but also models of animals, buildings and utensils in immense variety, intended for the equipment of the dead. The glaze on these wares contains lead and is in fact so similar to the green and yellow glazes on a certain class of Roman pottery appearing about the time of Christ (compare p. 22) that it was at one time assumed that in this matter the Chinese were borrowers from the West; through the overland silk trade which gave the name of their race to this material in Greek, Latin and derivative languages, they were already in contact with the Roman world. Recent discoveries, however, as has been hinted above, seem to show that this theory is untenable, and the question lotus-flower in the middle surrounded by formal clouds on a dappled background. It may be here pointed out that the Buddhist religion, introduced from India, received official recognition in China in A.D. 67 and continued to flourish under the T'ang emperors, spreading Buddhist symbolism, so that the lotus became an all-pervading motive in art. Traces of the Hellenistic influence which Buddhism carried with it eastward may also be seen in T'ang pottery as, for instance, in the adoption as a form of the Greek *œnochoe* (compare p. 14).

The Golden Age of Chinese pottery was the period of the Sung dynasty, synchronizing with the earlier Middle Ages in Europe. Porcelain then attained as a form of art a perfection which later technical refinements and developments never enabled it to surpass. It is the custom to classify the Sung porcelains in groups named after their places of production, but recent excavations tend to show that many of the types were not confined to any one locality but were the common stock of all, though they may have originated in the places from which they take their names. In all the best may be seen the same incomparable sensitiveness to formal values, combined with technical refinement of the highest order. Sung is the age particularly of low-toned glazes of exquisite texture carried by shapes displaying the subtlest beauty of profile.

Foremost of the Sung porcelains in their wide distribution outside China are the types developed from the Yüeh ware of earlier times, with a glaze ranging from sea-green to olive-green, which are now known in Europe as celadon (apparently for no better reason than that an actor impersonating a character of that name on the French stage in the eighteenth century wore a costume of this colour, which imported Chinese porcelain had then made fashionable). Celadon glazes undoubtedly won their never diminished popularity

PLATE VI

B. Stoneware jar, Chinese, Tz'ŭ-chou
(Page 58)

A. Porcelain bowl, Chinese, Lungch'üan
(Page 55)

(Victoria and Albert Museum)

in China because they gave to porcelain the outward
semblance of the highly-prized green jade; in India
and other countries celadon ware was much in favour
for its reputed antitoxic quality, being supposed to
break in pieces if poisoned food was served in it. The
first celadon was made in Sung times at Lungch'üan
in Chekiang province, and few things are lovelier to
sight and touch than some of the Lungch'üan dishes
and bowls with designs of fishes, lotus-flowers or birds,
engraved with exquisite mastery before the application
of the soft moss-green glaze (Plate VI, A). Another well-
marked kind was made apparently somewhere in Northern China and was much exported to the neighbouring
kingdom of Corea, where it was imitated by native
potters. It gave rise in Corea to two varieties of technique much practised in the fourteenth and fifteenth
centuries; one shows flowers or birds painted in a thick
greenish-black pigment under the celadon glaze; in
the other we find a technique apparently learnt in
China and passed on afterwards to Japan but characteristic above all of Corean porcelain—that of inlaying
the decoration by engraving it in the paste and then
filling the incision with black and white clay, the whole
finally receiving its outer dress of transparent green
glaze. Celadon porcelain imitating the Chinese was
also made about the same time in Siam and a good
deal later in Japan, whilst exports of it to the West
prompted Egyptian and Persian potters to emulation
with a celadon-coloured glaze on their coarse-bodied
earthenware.

Most highly prized of the Sung porcelains in China
itself were the kindred Ju and Kuan wares, made in the
twelfth century for Imperial use. They show pale
lavender, greyish or greenish glazes, in the case of
Kuan thick and rather opaque, with a wide " crackle "
of fissures caused by the unequal shrinking of the
" body " and glaze during firing (fig. 6). Ko is another
class of Sung crackled ware, but whitish to stone-grey

in colour and with crackle as a rule of much narrower mesh. These wares were for the most part devoid of decoration, so that their beauty of material and finish might make its appeal undisturbed. The large family of Ting wares, with a cream-white or pale straw-coloured glaze, includes many pieces which compete with the

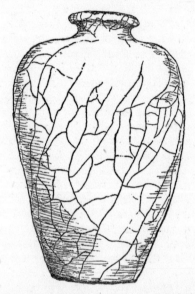

Fig. 6.—Porcelain vase, Chinese, Kuan ware (British Museum)

celadons and official wares for a high place in the artistic hierarchy. Like the celadons they often owe much of their beauty to the perfect composition and draughtsmanship shown in the lotus flowers, swimming ducks and other designs delicately engraved under the glaze; where reliefs produced by pressing in a mould have been employed, good as they are, they lack the spontaneity of engraving and fall into a lower category.

Less esteemed in China are the porcellanous stone-wares known as Chün and Chien, the former with a glaze which varies from a fiery crimson to deep lavender-blue or greenish-grey (fig. 7), including also a type in which crimson markings, sometimes irregular, sometimes in the form of a flower or a butterfly, have been deliberately obtained in the field of pale blue. The Chien wares, so named from being made amongst other places in the coast province of Fuchien, are no less varied in character, though in form consisting chiefly of conical or rounded tea-bowls. The archetype has a

Fig. 7.—Stoneware bowl, Chinese (Chün type)

thick deep brownish-black glaze usually marked with light brown flecks which have caused it to be likened to the fur of a hare. Amongst many other types are a plain dark brown, a rich dead-leaf brown, and a black showing thickly-clustered silvery spangles like spots of oil.

Lastly we come to a striking class of heavy, buff stoneware of vigorous masculine quality, made for more ordinary use. This ware is called after its places of production, Tz'ŭ-chou, in Chihlih province. It is seen mostly in massive bulbous jars or in large vases often of the slender egg-shape with small funnel neck made to contain a single spray of plum or other blossoming tree. The "body" is buff and the decoration various. In one class, perhaps the finest, the whole surface is thickly covered with the glaze, which fires to a dense dark brown, and the design, such as fishes or a frieze of lotus-flowers, is deeply engraved through the glaze before the ware is sent to the kiln for firing; the result of this technique is that, with the fusing of the glaze, the decoration stands out in slightly convex relief in the glaze-colour against the matt buff of the ground (Plate VI, B). In other kindred wares the ordinary *sgraffiato* technique is employed. Others again show sprays of peony or other flowers painted in black with the strong but subtle brush-strokes familiar in Chinese calligraphy, under a glaze which may be pale cream-colour or stained with copper to deep green; this class recalls the painted Corean celadon wares to which reference has been made above. Lastly, we occasionally find red and green enamel pigments, fixed at a second, low-temperature firing, added to these designs in black.

The Tz'ŭ-chou potteries have continued producing until the present day, but never again with the vitality shown in the wares made there (as proved by dates occasionally inscribed upon them) under the Sung emperors and during the short rule of the Mongol dynasty, known as Yüan, by which the last of them was conquered in 1279. Tz'ŭ-chou ware is of peculiar interest as the only important class of Sung pottery showing extensive use of painting as decoration. In ceramic history it is important as the forerunner of " blue-and-white ", the dominant type of Chinese porcelain of modern times, which seems already to have made its appearance on the scene before the fall of the Sung dynasty; but this is a development which will be dealt with in due course. We must relate first how glazing and painting were first combined, in Egypt, the motherland of the art of glass.

CHAPTER V

Egypt and the Near East;
Glaze and Painting

SOMETHING has been said already (p. 5) of the unglazed painted earthenware made in Egypt in pre-dynastic times. We must now take up the wonderful glazed ware which figures so conspicuously amongst all finds in Ancient Egyptian tombs. Glass was an Egyptian invention, and even before the beginning of the historic dynasties it seems to have occurred to the Egyptian craftsmen to apply it in the form of glaze to articles modelled or moulded in clay. Thus what is known from its colour as " Egyptian blue-glazed ware " came into existence. The oldest examples of it are moulded figurines of animals and birds, beads and other small articles; only at a later stage was it used on vessels. The glaze is a silicate of soda and lime; such an alkaline glaze could only be applied to a " body " containing itself a large proportion of silica mixed with the clay. In a material with so little cohesiveness, " largely " (as it has been said [1]) " sand held together by a little clay and glass," wheel-thrown pottery could not be made; the articles could only be kneaded together or pressed into moulds, perhaps held together by some gummy substance until the enclosing glaze had been fused into hardness by fire. Nevertheless in course of time quite large objects as

[1] By William Burton, *Encyclopædia Britannica*, 11th ed., Vol. V, 1910, " Ceramics ", p. 706.

well as many of great beauty were made in this manner.
One of the most astonishing achievements in blue-
glaze is the giant sceptre of the Eighteenth Dynasty in
the Victoria and Albert Museum, inscribed with the
name of King Amenhotep II (1449–1423 B.C.), which
stands seven feet high. For beauty may be named the
slender pale blue chalice of the Nineteenth Dynasty
(about 1350—1200 B.C.) with bowl moulded in the
shape of a lotus-flower, in the Ashmolean Museum,
Oxford.   Remarkable also are the round-bottomed
bowls painted with fishes and lotus-flowers which began
to appear during the Thirteenth Dynasty (eighteenth
century B.C.).

The Egyptian " blue glaze " is derived from copper
and varies from a very pale sky blue through intense
turquoise to a greenish tone. Already under the first
of the dynastic kings, Aha or Menes, we find manganese, producing a purplish-black colour, in use as a
pigment for inscribing names in hieroglyphics on
vases; they are painted on the blue glaze before it
is fired, fusing into the surface of the glaze with the
heat of the fire; this is an anticipation of the method
employed in painting the tin-enamelled earthenwares
of later times, with the difference that in the earlier
case the glaze is translucent, in the later opaque.
The same technique is employed in the painted bowls
of the Thirteenth Dynasty mentioned above and on
the remarkable figures of hippopotamuses of somewhat earlier date, with the reeds amongst which they
are lurking painted in purple on their bodies. During
the Eighteenth Dynasty (from about 1580 B.C.) we
find other coloured glazes in use besides the light blue,
including dark blue from cobalt, violet, red, yellow,
apple-green and white.   Under the Ptolemaic rulers
and in Roman times the " blue-glazed " technique
continued on traditional lines, but the wares under-
went a change of character in design under Hellenistic
influence. Noteworthy are the bowls and vases with

figures of deities or animals modelled in bold relief; particularly splendid in effect are certain jars, attributed to the first century after Christ, with festoons of laurel-leaves applied in sharp projection on the body and coloured with greenish-blue glaze in contrast with the rich plum-purple glaze of the ground.

The history of pottery in the Near East during the domination of Rome and the Eastern Empire is obscure, but although tangible proofs are few, there can be no doubt that in Egypt and Syria the technique of " blue-glazed ware " was kept alive. Although as we have seen (p. 22) various kinds of lead-glazed ware were also produced, the characteristic type of pottery throughout the Near East since the rise of Islam in the seventh century has been a ware of more or less coarse sandy " body " covered with a transparent siliceous glaze, with decoration either engraved under the glaze or painted. A " body " of this nature is of indifferent plasticity and incapable of being thrown on the wheel in thin or subtle shapes, but the siliceous glaze, as Ancient Egyptian examples amply prove, can be endowed by staining oxides with unsurpassed richness of colour, and lends great brilliance and intensity to underlying pigments seen through it.

Unbroken specimens from the earlier centuries of Islam are not numerous, but the character and diversity of the wares then made are proved by the thousands of potsherds found at Fostat (Old Cairo) and in excavations on many sites in Syria, Mesopotamia, Persia and Central Asia. Amongst these sites Samarra, the one-time residence of the Abbasid Caliphs, near Bagdad, which has already been mentioned in connexion with Chinese porcelain, is of peculiar interest to the archæologist because it is known that the place was only occupied for a limited period falling within the ninth century. Classification by localities, unless " wasters " from kilns proving local origin are amongst the finds, is a matter of difficulty, because there was traffic to and

fro throughout the Islamic world, from Spain to
Samarkand, and the same varieties of wares occur in
widely distant places. There is evidence also to prove
that certain techniques were practised with almost
indistinguishable results in more than one country.

The finds at Samarra, dating as we have seen, from
the eighth century, give us the earliest certain proofs
as to Islamic pottery, and here already we find in
practice a technique which was to have an immense
expansion in later times. A transparent siliceous glaze
necessitates, for fine brushwork, a previous coating of
the coarse " body " with a layer of white pipeclay to
provide a good painting-surface, but an alternative
procedure, already in evidence amongst the wares dug
up at Samarra, was to add to the glaze itself some
substance which would render it opaque and white,
so that the painting could be carried out upon it,
before firing, instead of under it (that is, before its
application). In later times the opacifying material
employed was oxide of tin, the use of which seems
already to have been known in the sixth century B.C.,
if the enamel on the bricks at Babylon and Susa is of
this order; a glaze of this nature is generally called a
tin enamel, but in the opaque glaze of these earlier
wares no trace of tin has been discovered by analysis.
The painting on the opaque-glazed earthenware from
Samarra is of two kinds, and the fact that on rare
examples both are combined shows that both types of
ware were made in the same workshops, which, it
has been suggested, are more likely to have been in
the great city of Bagdad, not far distant, than at
Samarra itself. In one class the designs are in cobalt
blue, often alone, but sometimes combined with bright
green; purple pigment also occurs. The motives of
decoration employed include rosettes, wreaths of
laurel and other foliage designs in which a late Hellenistic influence seems to be traceable.

The second class of painted ware from Samarra

PLATE VII

A. Vase, blue-glazed ware, Ancient
Egypt (Mr. D. Kelekian)
(Page 60)

B. Earthenware jug, Turkish, Isnik
(Victoria and Albert Museum)
(Page 67)

C. Earthenware bowl, *minai*, Persian, Rages. (Victoria and Albert Museum)
(Page 64)

gives us the earliest certain examples of painting in
metallic lustre pigments, the iridescent colours which
are the glory of the lustred wares made later in many
parts of the Near East as well as in Spain and Italy.
Lustre pigments are laid on the glaze or enamel when
it has already been fired; they require for their fixing
and for the development of the wonderful rainbow
hues resulting from the extreme thinness of the metal
deposit, a further firing and submission to a dense
smoke. The metals used are silver, giving brassy,
golden or lemon-yellow tones, or copper, producing
brownish tones or brilliant ruby-red; the two are
sometimes combined. Lustred wares exactly like those
from Samarra have been found in Egypt and at Susa,
in Persia, and the question whether distribution from
one centre, or imitative production in several, is the
explanation of this fact is one which still exercises
archæologists. In the earlier lustred wares we find
curious tree and leaf designs against a background of
cells containing spots or striped patterns suggestive
of interwoven palm-fronds; in these, two tones of
lustre, olive-green and brownish, are often combined.
Later there developed designs, including human figures
and animals, in " contour panels " (compartments,
that is, following the outline of the figure) reserved in
a diaper of large spots; this system of contour panelling
continued long in favour with Islamic pottery-painters
and was passed on in turn by them to Italy. One
of the most striking of these lustred wares is a bowl
in the Louvre painted with a mother camel suckling
her calf.

Lustre painting was practised with splendid effect
in Egypt, especially in the tenth and eleventh centuries
under the rule of the Fatimite sultans. The designs
range from birds and animals, to lute-players and other
human figures; a fragment in the Arab Museum at
Cairo with a head of Christ, and a bowl in the Kelekian Collection with a figure of a priest swinging a

censer, show that such wares were sometimes made for
Christian use and probably by native Copts. In the
twelfth and thirteenth centuries we find lustre-painting
of a high order in Persia, at Kashan and at Raay (the
Rages of the *Book of Tobit*[1]); highly characteristic are
the bowls and dishes with cavalcades of huntsmen or
princely figures squatting on thrones between female
attendants (Plate VII, c). Exactly similar designs were
painted, also over an opaque enamel,[2] in polychrome
pigments; these *minai* wares, as they are called, are
closely akin to the miniatures in Persian manuscripts
of the period.

At Rakka in Syria about the same time a somewhat
different class is found in which the lustre pigment,
usually brownish crimson in hue, is applied over a
thick transparent siliceous glaze, often of distinct
greenish tone. The designs show a boldness and vigour
which distinguish them from the suave, alluring
compositions of the Persian painters; they are repeated
also on another class of ware from Rakka, with painting in cobalt blue and black on white slip under the
glaze.   Such black-and-blue under-glaze painting became common also as the thirteenth century advanced,
and in the fourteenth, in Egypt and Persia, and in the
fifteenth century monochrome blue designs executed
in the same manner show not only in technique but
also in their motives the influence of Chinese blue-
and-white porcelain, which was then being brought in
shiploads to Western Asia and Africa. Mention must
here be made also very briefly of the splendid painting
in dense black under a transparent glaze (colourless,
or dark blue, turquoise, green or purple) of which many
of the best twelfth century potsherds from Fostat are
examples, whilst a similar technique in Persia (at
Kashan) produced some of the loveliest wares of the

[1] See R. Ettinghausen, "Evidence for the identification of Kāshān pottery ",
in *Ars Islamica*, III, p. 44.

[2] Analysis of a sample of *minai* ware from Raay in the Victoria and Albert
Museum has shown that the enamel contains tin.

thirteenth century (fig. 8); designs, such as that of a
running man on a bowl at South Kensington, are
thickly painted in black, with deeply incised details,
under a deep turquoise glaze, or again the whole surface
of a jug or bowl may be coated with black slip and the
decoration—an Arabic inscription or merely vertical
stripes—cut away through it so as to show blue through
the glaze. Egyptian and Syrian wares of this class as
well as lustred ware made their way to Italy as early

Fig. 8.—Earthenware bowl, Persian (Victoria and Albert Museum)

as the twelfth century, brought either by traders or
by returning Crusaders; they were used as architectural decoration, either in the brickwork of church
towers and gables or as elements in mosaic on screens
and pulpits.[1] They were not without influence on the
design of the Italian wares known as maiolica (compare
p. 85). Lastly there are the wares made in Egypt
and Persia in the twelfth and thirteenth centuries,
doubtless under the influence of imported Chinese
celadon and Ting ware (see p. 56), with designs boldly
carved into a fine white " body " and then, like the
painted wares, covered with a rich transparent coloured

[1] Compare G. Ballardini, " ' Bacini ' orientali a Ravello ", in *Bollettino
d'Arte*, 1934, p. 391.

glaze; here whilst animals and occasionally human figures play a conspicuous part, nothing is finer in effect than the employment, against a background of leafy scrollwork, of Arabic inscriptions in the noble type of lettering known from the city where it originated as Cufic.

During the fifteenth century Near Eastern pottery in general was at a low ebb, but it had a splendid rebirth in the sixteenth century, first in Turkey and somewhat later in Persia. The centre of production of the finer Turkish wares was Isnik (the Nicea of the Creed), in Anatolia; most of the craftsmen who made them were probably not Turks but Armenians, and there is record of potters introduced from Persia by the Sultan Selim I, in 1514. At Nicea was made, for some decades beginning towards the end of the sixteenth century, a fine earthenware with a thin glaze over a milk-white slip giving a porcelain-like appearance, with painting in cobalt blue. The motives of design consist chiefly of interlaced arabesques or Arabic inscriptions in Cufic characters set amongst an all-over pattern of flowers and leafy scrolls in which Chinese influence is unmistakable. Some of the finest examples are giant bowls on a high foot, like large salad-bowls. Blue-and-white ware of this kind was formerly attributed, owing to misinterpretation of an inscription, to Kutahia, a city which in the eighteenth century produced earthenware of very different character, largely for the use of Armenian Christians.

Soon after 1500 more naturalistic flowers begin to make their appearance in the decoration, and new colours, olive and emerald green, pale turquoise blue and deep manganese purple, with black, are added to the blue hitherto used almost exclusively, and the blue takes on a more intense tone, whilst the exquisite porcelain-like texture of the ware continues. Decoration begins to be predominantly floral and to

include, besides palmettes derived from the Chinese
lotus, others such as tulips, hyacinths, roses and
carnations, in forms only slightly modified from those
of nature. This class of ware, made about the middle
of the sixteenth century, had a strong influence, both
in colour and design, on the decorative compositions
of William Morris and his potter-collaborator, William
De Morgan, to whom it was known, in accordance
with the conceptions of their time, as Persian; a subsequent attribution, equally mistaken, was to Damascus, where later in the sixteenth century wares were
made with kindred design but less finely painted and
covered with a thick uneven glaze, often marred by
the greenish tone which is equally characteristic of
the mediæval Syrian wares from Rakka and elsewhere. The great bowls continued to be made at
Isnik, with the new themes and colouring; of these,
however, no finer example could be named than the
lamp with a date corresponding to A.D. 1549 from the
Mosque of Omar at Jerusalem, now in the British
Museum. On this lamp we still have arabesque inter-
lacements combined with inscriptions playing the chief
rôles, with small tulips in narrow bands as accessories.

From this " purple " family there blossomed at
Isnik, in the second half of the sixteenth century, the
magnificent ware so long known by a misnomer as
" Rhodian " (Plate VII, B). Its chief glory is the use,
in combination with deep blue, emerald green and
black, of a vermilion red never since surpassed in brilliance, obtained from an earth of which the quarry
seems in course of time to have been exhausted;
occasionally the slip providing the ground for this
painting is stained light or dark blue or salmon-colour,
in which case white slip pigment is added to the palette.
Flowers, cypress-trees and long serrated leaves, arranged sometimes symmetrically, always with well-
balanced rhythm, still dominate the painters' repertory,
but birds and animals are occasionally found, and

rarely, in late examples, human figures; at the same
time some of the most effective designs are entirely
conventional, such as well-graduated scale-pattern and
arabesques. The shapes of the wares include dishes,
jugs, tankards and long-necked bulbous bottles, always
of substantial build well suited to the graceful but
firm lines of the painting. As the seventeenth century
advanced there was a perceptible falling off in the
Isnik pottery; designs became weaker and confused
and the colours no longer had the purity which at their
best lent them such distinction.

The Persian renaissance began in the sixteenth
century, when there was a revival of lustre painting
widely different in character from that of the mediæval
workshops. The articles so decorated were small—
cups, rose-water bottles, spittoons, and flower-vases
with several apertures—and the glaze was often
stained to a beautiful intense blue on which the rainbow hues of the metallic pigment show up with brilliant
effect; amongst the designs irises, small cypress-trees
and willows are conspicuous. In the reign of the en-
lightened Shah Abbas the Great, the contemporary of
Queen Elizabeth and James I, Persian art in general
was at a high level and there was a wonderful development of pottery, shown in wares of fine quality and
great variety. Conspicuous amongst them is the fine
blue-painted earthenware, sometimes partly translucent, made in emulation of the Chinese porcelain
then being brought in large quantities to Persia. Literal
copies are the exception; as a rule Chinese themes
are adapted in a romantic mood very different from
that of the originals. The sinuous rhythms of Persian
art are seen at their best in depicting the stealthy
movements of the cheetah or the nervous spring of
the gazelle, or in occasional renderings of human figures
in subjects entirely free from Chinese influence.

It would be impossible to survey in detail the many
beautiful and varied types of ware made in Persia in

the seventeenth century. Besides the large class of
" blue-and-white ", the designs on which are often
outlined in black, there is another painted class in
which Chinese elements are seldom present; here, in
addition to a vivid cobalt blue, thick buff and bright
red slip pigments are used (the latter almost rivalling
the scarlet of the Isnik wares). Sometimes a coloured
slip, blue-stained or buff, is laid over the surface as a
ground for the painting of such themes as peacocks
or gazelles confronted on either side of a cypress or a
group of cornflowers, in opaque white and other colours.
In a lovely variety, of which a deep blue rice-dish
in the Victoria and Albert Museum engraved with a
branch of willow is an example hardly to be surpassed for its restrained effectiveness, the decoration
is not painted over the coloured slip but cut through
it so as to reveal the underlying white " body ", in
the manner of the lead-glaze *sgraffiato* wares (compare
p. 27).

Entirely different in technique are the wares with
monochrome glazes, deep cucumber-green, olive-green,
celadon, turquoise or dark blue and rich amber-yellow,
made in emulation of " self-coloured " Chinese porcelain
(compare p. 78); sometimes these have moulded relief
designs of plant-forms and animals (a cheetah in leash
with its keeper, for instance) displaying to the full the
simplified rhythms characteristic of Persian art. In
all these later Persian wares the glaze is of the pre-
dominant Near Eastern class, a glassy siliceous glaze
requiring a considerable proportion of sand in the
composition of the " body ".

CHAPTER VI

Far Eastern Painted Porcelain

CHINESE porcelain in its modern and most familiar form began to emerge about the end of the Sung period. Specimens painted in blackish cobalt blue—with ducks swimming amongst lotuses and other Buddhist themes—under a greyish-white glaze of semi-opaque, milky appearance, have been attributed to this period on the evidence of finds in graves believed to date therefrom. In the brushwork they are closely akin to the painted Tz'ŭ-chou stoneware of Sung and Yüan times (compare p. 57), the pigment being freely applied without preliminary outlines (fig. 9). Whatever their age, they are the earliest examples of the use in China of cobalt as a pigment for graphic designs; it had been so used, as we have seen (p. 62), in the Near East in the ninth century, whilst its appearance about the same period in China as a material for staining glazes had been anticipated long before in Eighteenth Dynasty Egypt. The best quality of cobalt was known in China as "Mohammedan blue", and the source from which it was obtained, when the trade routes were not interrupted by war or other commotions, was somewhere in Western Asia, probably in Persia or Baluchistan. All uncertainty as to date disappears with a pair of tall blue-and-white altar-vases, in private possession,[1] which are decorated with the Imperial dragon and phœnixes, and bands filled with lotus and

[1] Reproduced in Hobson, Rackham and King, *Chinese Ceramics in Private Collections*, London, 1931 (fig. 292).

other flowers; these vases have inscriptions dating them to the year A.D. 1352, when an emperor of the Mongolian Yüan dynasty was on the throne of China. Soon after, in 1368, this dynasty was displaced by the native Ming dynasty, which endured until, in 1643, it was in turn overthrown by Manchu conquerors.

One of the earliest acts of the first Ming emperor,

Fig. 9.—Blue-and-white early ewer

Hung Wu, was the establishment of an Imperial porcelain factory in the ancient pottery town of Ching-tê-chên, near the Poyang lake, which empties into the Yangtse some 450 miles above Nanking. This factory, intended for supplying the needs of the Court at Nanking (later transferred to Peking) became the model for technique and style in the scores of other workshops carried on in the town. A word may be said here as to the chief characteristics of Ching-tê-chên porcelain. It is pure white and translucent, with a colourless glaze so nearly akin in composition to the

" body " that, in firing, the two coalesce where they
are in contact, without any sharp division; to this the
ware owes its pellucid, snowlike brilliance and the blue
pigment its depth of tone. For the colouring of the
ware three principal classes of technique are employed.
Certain colours will withstand the high firing-tempera-
ture of porcelain and can therefore be laid as pigments
on the unfired surface of the " body " before application
of the glaze, or used to stain the glaze itself, " body "
and glaze being then submitted at a single operation
to their only firing in the kiln; these colours include
besides the cobalt of " blue-and-white ", a celadon-
green and a russet (" dead-leaf ") brown, both obtained
from iron, and a crimson derived from copper, which
in certain conditions of temperature may turn to liver-
colour or warm grey, or develop green markings which
have been likened to those of the bloom on a peach.
It may here be remarked that the unfired surface,
whether the " body " itself, as in Chinese porcelain,
or a slip or tin enamel as on the various classes of
Near Eastern earthenwares described in Chapter V,
and their European descendants, is porous and absor-
bent; painting on it is consequently like painting on
blotting-paper and calls for long practice and dexterity,
for when once a line has been made with the brush
there can be no erasure or wiping out. A second range
of colours are in the nature of stained glaze-pigments
containing lead in their composition; these are laid on
the ware when it has already been fired to what is
known as the " biscuit " state, and require a further
firing at a moderate temperature for fixing them.
Pigments of this order were often employed in Ming
times over a " body " which is in the nature rather of
stoneware than of true porcelain. The third principal
class of pigments consists of those known as " enamel
colours ", that is to say, mixed with a soft glassy
flux, easily fused, and applied over the usual colourless
glaze after the first firing of the ware; like those of the

last class, these colours, which may also be used as monochrome enamel-glazes, necessitate a second firing, but at a very low temperature in what is known as a " muffle " kiln. Gilding is fixed in porcelain in the same manner.

All these various processes were in practice at Ching-tê-chên as early as the fifteenth century and have continued so to the present day. Though later times witnessed many advances in technical skill and a great expansion in the repertory of designs available to the painters, no period has shown more consummate artistry than the short reign of the art-loving Hsüan Tê (1426–1435). Specimens of this time are of great rarity (Plate VIII, A), but many are to be found inscribed under the base with the six-character mark of Hsüan Tê's reign; the same applies to that of another famous fifteenth century emperor, Ch'êng Hua. The explanation of this is that it became the custom in after times to use the names of famous bygone emperors not only on wares reproducing the styles of their periods but indiscriminately, as a consequence of the Chinese veneration for ancestors and the men of old. Thus the names of these two early Ming emperors are common on eighteenth century porcelain, whilst the occurrence of that of the eighteenth century K'ang Hsi must also be viewed with suspicion, as it has been very popular with the potters of Ching-tê-ch'ên on wares of inferior quality made in quite recent times.

The Ming wares cover a vast range of types; to pass them all in review here would be impossible. At one end of the scale we have the delicate little bowls and wine-cups of the fifteenth century, painted with tiny figures in a mountain landscape or lotus scrolls or a few scattered blossoms and butterflies, either in an even wash of soft pale blue within a linear outline, or in the "five-colour" scheme consisting of the same under-glaze blue and four enamel colours—

green, mauve, yellow and red; at the other end we
find, for instance, the massive wine-jars and fish-
bowls with powerful dragon designs or landscapes in
the dark blue, perhaps combined with intense enamel
colours, characteristic of the reign of Chia Ching
(1522–1566), and the ewers and large rice-dishes in
blue-and-white of his grandson, Wan Li, which so
strongly influenced Persian pottery (compare p. 68),
and made their way in numbers even to Europe. One
or two pieces of earlier blue-and-white or celadon
with late Gothic European silver mounts survive to
show how highly such rarities were prized in the West;
but it was not till the Dutch and English East India
Companies opened up a regular direct trade that
Chinese porcelain became a customary article of import
and as such imposed imitation of Oriental designs on
the pottery-painters of Europe.

These blue and polychrome painted porcelains
represent the revolutionary contribution of the Ming
period to the development of the art in China. There
were other types, however, which deserve mention
with almost equal honour as part of the great Ming
achievement. Single-colour glazes continued to appear,
following Sung precedents. Celadon ware, made now
especially at Ch'u-chou, was largely exported to India
and Western Asia, chiefly in the form of heavy bowls
and rice-dishes with floral designs boldly incised or
stamped under the glaze. From the Imperial kilns
came stem-cups for ritual use (with tall, slightly tapering foot) and water-pots for moistening the writer's
brush, with a deep crimson copper glaze which was to
inspire to worthy emulation the eighteenth century
craftsmen; on some cups of this form the same copper
red is used as a pigment for painting prescribed designs
such as three fishes. A very noble group is that of the
wares, often of a somewhat coarse stoneware " body "
which was particularly favourable to the development of the colours, with painting " on the biscuit "

PLATE VIII

A. Porcelain bowl, blue-and-white, Chinese
(Page 73)

B. Porcelain dish, *famille verte*, Chinese
(Page 77)
(Both, Victoria and Albert Museum)

in rich coloured glazes—dark blue, turquoise, deep aubergine-purple, and straw-yellow. The designs—for which lotus and chrysanthemum sprays or scenes from the life of mountain philosopher-hermits were greatly in favour — are either engraved in the paste or laid on in " slip " in slightly raised outline, like the metal strips in *cloisonné* enamel; the purpose in both cases is to prevent the overflow of the readily fused glaze-pigments applied as flat washes within the outlines. This technique was especially and suitably chosen for making large heavy articles such as wine-jars, flower-pots and barrel-shaped garden seats; the finest of these date from the fifteenth century.

The troubles which befell the empire in the seventeenth century account for a decline of quality in the latest Ming wares, but there was a glorious revival before the century closed in the reign of the second emperor of the Manchu dynasty, the great K'ang Hsi (1662–1722). When peace had been restored in the realm K'ang Hsi turned his attention to the encouragement of every form of artistic activity, and one of his foremost concerns was the imperial porcelain factory. This he rebuilt and placed under the charge of an energetic director whose business it should be to revive and surpass the splendid achievements of the past. The result was an enormous expansion of the industry in general, so that the number of kilns at Ching-tê-chên is said to have increased tenfold.

In perfection of technique K'ang Hsi porcelain at its best represents the peak of ceramic attainment. Past processes were revived and many new ones introduced, but technical excellence was apt to be sought at the cost of artistic quality. Shape and design tend to be obscured by an excess of meticulously painted detail. In the painting of birds and flowers there was an increasing trend towards naturalism. In landscape the K'ang Hsi painters were more ambitious than their Ming predecessors; some of their most notable successes were in this branch, in which they followed not so much earlier modes in porcelain as the pictures on silk of the great Sung school of landscape-painting.

Under K'ang Hsi there was an enormous development of " blue-and-white ". The cobalt pigment is very various in tone and sometimes surpasses in the purity of its intense sapphire hue anything attained before; it was laid on, not in even washes within darker outlines as in Ming times, but in graded tones to which the light penetrating the glaze gives an effect of throbbing vitality. It is seen at its best on the wrongly so-called " hawthorn jars ", similar in shape to the common ginger-jars of the modern grocer's shop. They were made to contain New Year's gifts of tea or sweetmeats and were appropriately decorated with the emblems of that season (falling in March by the Chinese calendar)—branches of blossoming plum (not may) against a blue ground with a network of lines intended to represent the cracking ice of winter departing. This is only one of the immense repertory of designs at the disposal of the porcelain-painters. Some were developed, and many new shapes were introduced, specially for the taste of European buyers within whose reach the wares were brought chiefly by the enterprise of Dutch merchants; in due course both shapes and designs were copied or travestied in the European factories. Among the types so made for the western market are the vases in sets of five— *garnitures de cheminée*—consisting generally of three baluster vases with lids and two beakers to match. For these and for tea-table wares a design very popular in Holland consists of slender figures of ladies standing alone, in panels of lotus-petal shape with sprays of flowers in intervening panels; they were known in Dutch as *lange leisjes* (" gawky lasses ") and in England by corruption as " Long Elizas ".

The great glory of the imperial factory in this reign

was undoubtedly the enamel-painted porcelain.   The
more numerous class is that with over-glaze painting,
in which colour effects of unrivalled brilliance were
attained.   The palette of the Ming " five-colour "
porcelain was extended to include many intermediate
shades, and under-glaze blue was supplanted in the
latter part of the reign by a blue enamel, sometimes
inclining to a violet tone. The design was first painted
in black outline—not, as formerly, under-glaze blue—
within which the enamel pigments were afterwards
applied. Green of varied shades dominates the scheme,
whence the term *famille verte*, the name given by
French connoisseurs, is commonly used to describe this
whole class of porcelain.   The colour-scheme is seen
at its loveliest in compositions of flowers and birds,
but it was employed for subjects of every possible
kind including illustrations of Chinese romances and
plays, often crowded with figures in expressive and
animated gestures.   Amongst the most charming of all
famille verte motives are the exquisitely drawn figures
of ladies in gardens, sometimes alone, sometimes
playing with children (Plate VIII, B).

A second class of K'ang Hsi enamelled porcelain is
that in which, following another Ming precedent,
coloured lead glazes were used as pigments laid, not
over an already fired colourless glaze like the enamels
of the *famille verte*, but directly on the unglazed biscuit
" body ".   The K'ang Hsi wares of this class mostly
display a combination of various greens with yellow
and mauve; the results are peculiarly happy when
such a scheme is enlisted for rendering mountain
landscapes. A famous group in this kind of technique
is that of the vases, often of large size, with compositions mostly of flowers or blossoming trees standing
out against an intense black ground; this lustrous black
is obtained by laying a wash of the dry black pigment
used also for drawing the outlines of the composition
and then flooding it over with a transparent green.

One of the tasks set by K'ang Hsi to the imperial factory was the revival of the famous coloured glazes of Sung and early Ming times. Some of these " self-coloured " wares rank beside those of the *famille verte* as the finest achievements of the time. Foremost is the crimson derived from copper in tones ranging from powerful *sang-de-bœuf* to the soft green-dappled tones of " peach bloom " and the various shades of liver-colour; as in Ming times, the same colour was also used as an under-glaze pigment, now for the first time often in combination with cobalt blue and celadon green. Cobalt is present in the pale lavender-blue and *clair-de-lune* glazes; it was also sometimes sprayed on to the " body " through a gauze-covered tube, before the application of a colourless glaze, to form " powder blue ", over which designs in gold were commonly painted. " Powder blue " is also seen on vases with panels reserved in white in which are flower or landscape paintings done in blue or in *famille verte* enamels. Excellent celadon green (often over engraved designs emulating those of Sung porcelain), " dead-leaf brown " and " mirror black " are other high-temperature mono-chrome glazes of the period. The gorgeous *rouge flambé* crimson mottled with purple was not introduced until the time of K'ang Hsi's grandson, Ch'ien Lung. The chief low-temperature glazes were imperial yellow, coral red, apple green and turquoise blue. Mention may be made here also of the plain white porcelain known as " blanc de Chine ", varying in colour from ivory to pure snow-white; this was the speciality from the seventeenth century onwards of potteries at Tê-hua, in Fuchien province, one of the few centres which continued to make porcelain of fine quality after the concentration of the industry in early Ming times round the imperial factory at Ching-tê-chên.

K'ang Hsi was succeeded by his son Yung Chêng, who was followed after a reign of twelve years by Ch'ien

Lung; the last-named emperor abdicated in the 60th year of his rule, 1795, as an act of piety, to avoid out-reigning his illustrious grandfather. Under Yung Chêng and Ch'ien Lung wares of fine quality continued to be produced, and new processes were adopted, but whilst technical skill was maintained porcelain as an art declined. Careful copies of Ming blue-and-white and enamelled wares were made, especially by order of Ch'ien Lung, who was an enthusiastic admirer of ancient art. The only important innovation of the period was the introduction from Europe of a rose-pink enamel, which had already made its appearance shortly before the death of K'ang Hsi. It is seen at its best in the famous ruby-backed eggshell plates with paintings of ladies and children, cocks and hens, or flowers, enclosed by multiple diaper borders, sometimes of seven different patterns. The dominant pink has won for the enamelled porcelain of this phase the name of *famille rose*; in inferior quality made for export it was brought to Europe and faithfully copied, particularly in the English factories during their earliest stages. A new development was the establishment of enamelling workshops in Canton to which plain white porcelain was sent from the commercial factories at Ching-tê-chên to be decorated with heraldic and other designs, after patterns sent out from Europe through the agency of the various East India companies.

Japan stands to a large extent apart from the general trend of ceramic development. The Japanese were from early times enthusiastic admirers of ancient Chinese and Corean wares, not least of the more robust types of porcellanous stoneware; from this preference the native art in the sixteenth and seventeenth centuries tended towards the production in numerous small workshops of stoneware, in the form especially of tea-bowls and other vessels intended for use at tea-ceremonies and showing a strongly individual character.

Of the many minor porcelain factories in Japan it would be impossible to speak here; brief mention must be made only of a heavy type made at Kutani, in the province of Kaga. Designs on old Kutani ware are mostly either in monochrome iron red or in a harmonious palette of enamel colours of great intensity—dark violet, deep green, yellow and black. The decoration—trees, fruit or flowers—is conceived in a mood almost of vehemence, in keeping with the massive quality of the ware and the powerful colouring.

PLATE IX

B. Maiolica plate, by Nicola Pellipario, Italian
(*Page 88*)
(Royal Scottish Museum, Edinburgh)

A. Back of lustred dish, Spanish
(*Page 85*)
(Victoria and Albert Museum)

CHAPTER VII

Maiolica, Delft and Faïence

MENTION has already been made (p. 65) of the painted bowls from the Near East used by Italian builders in the twelfth century and later to embellish their architecture, and there is evidence as early as the tenth century of lustred pottery imported into the south of Spain. From these beginnings grew the great art of earthenware with painting on a tin enamel in Spain and Italy, and later in other parts of Europe. Ware of this type was made also in Provence in the fourteenth century, and painted tiles with a tin enamel were used, and apparently made, at Utrecht in the same period,[1] but these seem to be isolated cases, unconnected with later developments in France and the Netherlands.

In the twelfth century an Arab geographer speaks of " golden " pottery made in Aragon which can hardly be other than lustred ware; this is the first clear evidence of such ware produced in Spain. In the fourteenth century we have the earliest tangible as distinct from literary documents. To this period belong the famous lustred vase in the Alhambra and the other rare examples of the same type scattered in various museums; they are all of considerable size, with pear-shaped body drawn almost to a point at the lower end, ribbed funnel-shaped neck and two handles rising from

[1] See *Faenza*, IX, 1921, p. 84; X, 1922, p. 25, R. de Cabrens, " La céramique gothico-mauresque dans le sud-est de la France "; *Faenza*, XXI, 1933, p. 131, F. W. Hudig, " Maiolica olandese del Trecento ".

the shoulder and shaped like the fins of a shark. They are painted in golden lustre with intricate designs showing great variety in detail but certain elements in common, such as bands of Arabic inscription and interlaced arabesques; on the Alhambra vase pairs of confronted gazelles are introduced among the ornament. These vases were doubtless made at or near Granada. A lustred bowl in Berlin, with arabesque ornament of similar style, seems from an inscription on it to have come from Malaga.

In the fifteenth century the manufacture of lustred pottery became concentrated at Manises, near Valencia. A thriving pottery industry had long existed in the neighbouring town of Paterna, where in the fourteenth century enamelled earthenware was made with decoration of strongly Gothic character—human figures, birds, fishes and trees, amongst other motives—painted in manganese-purple, with copper-green for filling in details; the same technique was being used at the same period in Italy, whilst in Spain it survived into the sixteenth century, with considerable change of style, at Teruel, in Aragon. The Manises lustre ware quickly rose to the front rank of artistic importance and was so much esteemed that it was exported as far afield as England and Holland in the north and Cairo in the east; some of the finest examples were made to order for Italy, with shields of arms of Venetian and Florentine families. Drug-pots and large dishes make up a large proportion of the wares. The decoration is painted in lustre, at first brownish or golden, in the later period of a rich copper red, generally accompanied by blue. At first mock Arabic inscriptions repeating benedictory formulas played a leading rôle. Towards the middle of the fifteenth century various stock patterns were adopted, of high decorative value, based on the foliage and tendrils of the vine or bryony—especially on the superb dishes for Italian clients; in the best period these are often painted on the back with a large eagle (the emblem of St. John the Evangelist, patron of Valencia), a lion, fleur-de-lys or other ornament (Plate IX, A) almost surpassing in beauty the decoration on the front. After about 1500 there was a marked change of character and a rapid artistic decline; the designs are sometimes embossed, and acanthus foliage showing the influence of the Renaissance is common. The virtues of later Spanish pottery are to be sought in wares of an entirely different character, made in various places but especially at Talavera, which became the chief centre of the industry in the country. After a period in which Italian influence is obvious, the Talavera potters in the seventeenth century asserted their native character in the production of earthenware which makes up by the almost savage vitality of its decoration for a lack of technical refinement. Huge oil-jars, basins and dishes are covered with compositions —in one class in blue and reddish orange only, in another polychrome with a strong green as dominant— in which fantastic birds or animals amongst foliage, or bull-fighting and battle scenes are rendered in a vigorous style showing no taint of foreign bias. Of Spanish earthenware in the eighteenth century a word will be said later (compare p. 92).

The fourteenth century witnessed the development from earlier modest beginnings of the enamelled earthenware of Italy, commonly known as *maiolica*. The word, an Italian form of the name of Majorca, is a misnomer, due to the fact that ships from that island were engaged in carrying from Spain the Valencian lustred ware to which it was at first applied; its meaning was later extended to cover also Italian lustred ware in which the Spanish technique was adopted, and finally any kind of earthenware with painting on a tin enamel. The earliest Italian ware of the class we now call maiolica, painted like the Paterna ware (see p. 84), in purple with filling in green, is purely Gothic in character, with designs from the

animal and plant world, or heraldry, in the style then
current in other arts (fig. 10). Such wares have been
found in quantity at Orvieto but were also made in
many other cities of northern Italy. In the middle of
the fifteenth century potteries in Florentine territory,
probably at Montelupo, were taking the lead. Conspicuous amongst the early Florentine wares are the
oviform drug-pots with human figures or animals
amongst foliage like that of the oak, painted in purple
and in a blackish-blue pigment laid on so thickly as to
stand out in tangible relief. About 1450 the palette
was extended; a clearer blue appears, accompanied
by purple, green and yellow or orange, and these
colours are sometimes employed in designs which show
plainly the influence of the imported Valencian ware.

In the second half of the fifteenth century the lead
in the output of maiolica passed to the little city of
Faenza, in the Romagna, near Ravenna, and from its
name the word *faïence* has passed into French and
other languages. Amongst the forms of vessels made
in maiolica one of the most characteristic was now the
nearly cylindrical shape known as *albarello*, introduced
from Spain, generally inscribed with the name of the
intended contents (fig. 11). Before 1500 the maiolica
palette had assumed at Faenza a harmonious richness
and intensity unsurpassed in the history of pottery. The
earlier Faenza wares show a definitely Gothic character,
with powerful leaf motives or ornament inspired by
peacock's feathers, accompanying single figures of men
or animals treated in an intentionally decorative
manner. Late in the century, complex figure-subjects
begin to appear, at first within a border of leaves or
formal ornament. For such compositions we have seen
precedents in Near Eastern painted pottery; but other
influences were now subtly at work. On every side
the great masters of painting and their pupils were
plying their brushes on wall and easel-panel, and the
maiolica painters were quick to realize the possibilities

of emulation with pigments to which fusion in the kiln gave an enduring sheen and brilliance attainable by no other means. From decorative painting on pottery made for use they passed on, soon after 1500, to the use of earthenware dishes and tablets as recipients for frankly pictorial subjects, intended for decoration only. In some of these the influence of Mantegna, Perugino,

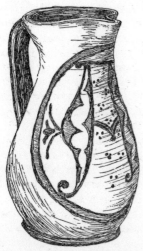 

Fig. 10.—Early Italian maiolica jug
(Victoria and Albert Museum)

Fig. 11.—Faenza maiolica drug-pot
(Victoria and Albert Museum)

Signorelli or Melozzo is clearly recognizable, and very soon the multiplication of prints by engravers such as Marcantonio Raimondi made easy the adaptation—often the slavish copying—of the works of Raphael and others.

The lead in this direction was given at Faenza by an anonymous painter who devoted himself mainly to religious subjects; his best-known work—a panel with the Resurrection, obviously inspired by one of Dürer's woodcuts—is in the Victoria and Albert Museum.

Meanwhile in the duchy of Urbino, at Castel Durante, a new school of maiolica painting was being established. In the first four decades of the sixteenth century a certain Giovanni Maria—or a painter working for a Durantine master-potter of that name, it is not certain which—painted bowls and plates with highly fanciful compositions, mostly quite original, in harmony with a mood of wistful detachment not untinged with cruelty and psychologically characteristic of this age in which new experience was being sought in every direction. This artist was followed by Nicola Pellipario, the most accomplished of all maiolica painters, whose versatile skill was proved both in decorative designs and in others, entirely pictorial, depicting subjects preferably drawn from Ovid and other ancient authors (Plate IX, B). He is essentially the pottery-painter of humanism. Whilst he owed much to book illustrations and engravings, which he sometimes copied closely, he was gifted with the power of endowing the motives he borrowed from them with a new attractiveness; he handled them with a charm and grace all his own, generally in a landscape setting in which the beauty of his colouring is seen at its best; nor was he incapable of entirely original composition on occasion.

Pellipario seems to have migrated, a little before 1530, from Castel Durante to the city of Urbino, where he was followed by a host of inferior pictorial painters; amongst them Francesco Xanto, known from his often-recurring signature, alone calls for mention on account of his robust and richly chromatic style. As to the technical processes of the Urbino workshops there is full information in the contemporary manuscript of Cipriano Piccolpasso, now in the Victoria and Albert Museum, the oldest extant European monograph on the art of the potter.

Maiolica was made in many other places. Siena was about 1500 the home of a certain Maestro Benedetto, whose work bears the mark of a simple religious sincerity. Deruta, near Perugia, was the first Italian pottery-centre to practise lustre painting. Here were produced in particular heavily built dishes with deep middle and broad rim painted in blue outline and pale brassy yellow lustre with portraits, heraldic shields, or sacred and allegorical subjects in which Franciscan influence from neighbouring Assisi can be discerned. From this Umbrian town the art of lustre-painting made its way into the duchy of Urbino—to Gubbio, where Maestro Giorgio Andreoli began about 1517 to produce maiolica resplendent with a brilliant ruby-red lustre never surpassed elsewhere. In Tuscany work of the highest standard was done about the same time by a painter named Jacopo in a workshop established at the castle of Caffaggiolo, near Florence, belonging to a branch of the Medici family; famous compositions of this artist (both at South Kensington) are his only signed work, Judith and her servant on horseback with the head of Holofernes, and a picture of himself decorating a plate in the presence of a patron and his lady. Lustred ware of fine quality was also made for a short time at Caffaggiolo.

Towards 1550 a change came over maiolica painting. There was a reaction against the pictorial manner then holding the field but manifestly with weakened power. At Urbino itself a new style was introduced, based on the grotesques painted by Raphael in the Loggie of the Vatican in emulation of the antique, in which the enamel was not entirely concealed by pigment but its creamy pleasantness was enhanced by a filigree of satyrs, sphinxes and winged genii giving wide scope to painters of whimsical imagination. Even more free and delightful in its effect was the style introduced about the same time at Faenza, where technical improvements had resulted in an enamel of gleaming whiteness; to display its excellence a slight decoration was adopted of simple figures of Cupid or of a saint encircled by a formal wreath, all sketchily painted in a low-toned scheme of colour, chiefly blue, orange and purplish-black. In addition to painted wares, Faenza took the lead, afterwards followed elsewhere, in supplying at low prices large quantities of plain white maiolica of good quality. Venice, which came to the fore, as a home of maiolica about 1540, had a manner of its own in which arabesques play an important part combined with figures or grotesques, mostly painted in dark blue and opaque white on an enamel stained with cobalt to a pale lavender grey; here and in contemporary wares from Caffaggiolo the influence of the Turkish pottery of Isnik (compare p. 66) was operative, and indirectly that of Chinese blue-and-white porcelain.

In the seventeenth century the maiolica industry was carried on in many new centres; chief amongst these was the district of Genoa and Savona, on the Ligurian coast. Chinese influence becomes more and more apparent, whilst figure composition conforms with the prevailing Baroque fashion, and moulded embossment in the manner of the silver plate of the period was often adopted. In the eighteenth century there was a revival of the pictorial style of Urbino, but with a very different chromatic tonality, especially at Siena, and at Castelli, in the Abruzzi, where a thriving maiolica industry had grown up; the compositions chosen by the painters were copied chiefly from the Carracci, Bassano and later masters. At the same time Faenza continued to be productive, adapting to maiolica painting themes derived from Chinese and Japanese porcelain. Towards the end of the century maiolica declined to the status of a peasant craft, under the stress of importation from England of fine earthenware which compelled Italian firms to turn their attention to the output of the same class of goods.

From Italy the art of maiolica was carried by emigrant potters beyond the Alps. Some went to Germany and Moravia, and to Switzerland, where they founded flourishing potteries at Winterthur. From 1512 onwards there are records of Italian potters settled at Lyons, although their earlier productions have not been identified; some inferior pictorial maiolica in the Urbino manner attributed to a Lyons workshop dates from the second half of the century. Maiolica drug-pots and pavement tiles with painting in French early Renaissance style are recognized as the work of a potter of French birth at Rouen; he is first recorded as owner of a pottery in 1543.[1] In 1585 an Italian potter from Albissola, near Genoa, was summoned by a syndicate to set up a factory at Nevers, and the important faïence industry still carried on in that city was founded;[2] it may here be explained that the word " faïence " should strictly speaking be used only, like " maiolica ", of earthenware with a tin enamel. The earliest Nevers ware is mostly polychrome, with mythological and other figure-subjects in colours which though powerful have not the rich diversity of those of early Italian maiolica. In the seventeenth century a more restrained and sober palette supervened, often limited to blue and dark purple, under the influence of imported Chinese porcelain, and Chinese subjects took their place amongst the themes of the decorators beside European hunting-scenes adapted from contemporary engravings. A class apart amongst the Nevers wares, imitated in England at Lambeth, are those with painting of flowers and birds or Chinese landscapes in opaque white over an enamel stained dark blue.

Towards 1700 an artistic decline set in at Nevers and the leadership in faïence passed to Rouen. For about half a century the numerous potteries of Rouen turned out wares of high quality. In the earlier stages,

---

[1] See *Les Amis de Sèvres*, *Bulletin No. 32*, 1938, p. 57, M. Dehlinger, " Abaquesne et son œuvre ".

[2] Not at the instance of the Duke, Louis de Gonzague, as usually stated; see G. Montagnon, " Origine della fabbricazione di faenze a Nevers ", in *Faenza*, XXV, 1937, p. 18.

gay palette of blue, orange, green and purple. Early
in the seventeenth century there was a fashion also
for grotesque designs derived, with considerable modi-
fication, from those originated at Urbino, and accompanying figures or landscapes obviously at home in
the country of Rembrandt.

About the middle of the seventeenth century various
circumstances led to the concentration of the Dutch
maiolica industry at Delft, and the word " delft " came
henceforward into currency as the name for tin-

Fig. 12.—Netherlandish maiolica vase (London Museum)

enamelled earthenware of the kind there made.
From the first there was a tendency at Delft to
discard the bright colours of the earlier maiolica
in favour of blue-and-white; the movement was due
to a variety of circumstances—for instance, the sombre
austerity common to Protestantism and the counter-
Reformation as shown in early Baroque art in general;
but most powerful of all influences was certainly that
of the porcelain which Dutch merchants were beginning
to import by shiploads from China. Much of the earlier
blue and white is delightfully painted with subjects in
the manner of the Dutch genre and landscape painters
of the day, notably the plates with rustic scenes in

PLATE X

B. Earthenware dish, Lambeth (Fitzwilliam
Museum, Cambridge)
(*Page* 97)

A. Earthenware bottle, Dutch, Delft (National
Gallery of Victoria, Melbourne)
(*Page* 95)

C. Faïence soup-tureen, French, Strasburg (Victoria and Albert Museum)
(*Page* 93)

blue, in a medallion surrounded by a wide border of
plain white, drawn by the skilful brush of Frederik van
Frÿtom; but more and more, fashion insisted upon
Eastern themes, sometimes copied with almost decep-
tive fidelity from Chinese porcelain, until about 1690,
when Delft ware was reaching the zenith of its technical
perfection, Chinese and Japanese designs are in the
majority; the monogram of the potter Samuel van
Eenhoorn is found under the base of many of the vases
and jugs of the finest quality made about this time
(Plate X, A). By the beginning of the eighteenth century, in emulation both of Imari ware and of K'ang
Hsi *famille verte* (compare pp. 81, 77), a polychrome
palette was coming once more into favour, but of a
very different order from that of the maiolica of the
past. To the four maiolica pigments, much softened in
tone, is now added an iron red, and in a favourite
class of Oriental designs this colour is accompanied
only by dark blue and gold. Almost throughout the
eighteenth century the Delft factories were kept busily
at work, with orders both for home and foreign buyers,
but their wares steadily declined in quality and consequently in their interest to the student and collector.

In the eighteenth century the faïence industry was
widespread in Germany. Maiolica was made in the
south, as we have seen, in the sixteenth century, and
from about 1620 for some thirty years there was a
factory at Hamburg, the most characteristic products
of which are blue-and-white wine-jugs painted with the
arms of the city; there was, however, no enduring
manufacture of tin-enamelled earthenware until, in
1661, two Dutch potters from Delft sought for a concession from the city council of Frankfort-on-the-
Main for the erection of a factory; they were refused
and set up business in the neighbouring town of Hanau,
but five years later the privilege they had sought in
vain at Frankfort was granted to a Frenchman in their
employ. The earlier Hanau and Frankfort wares are

sometimes difficult to distinguish from one another and from those of Delft. Characteristic of Frankfort is a bright blue used in painting Chinese themes, notably lotus-flowers and leaves treated with an easily recognizable mannerism.

After this beginning faïence factories sprang up in quick succession all over Germany. A typical German shape and no less typical baroque design were introduced in the potteries under the patronage of the Elector of Brandenburg at Potsdam and Berlin. This was the *Humpen* or cylindrical beer-tankard, made to be fitted with a pewter lid. For its decoration, early in the eighteenth century, symmetrical Baroque panelling was the rule, with a space on the front in which was introduced a crowned cipher or the Prussian eagle, painted in blue often against a background of " powdered " manganese purple. The type spread to other German potteries using high - temperature colours.

About 1750 the muffle pigments in imitation of porcelain-painting introduced at Strasburg (see p. 92) were adopted in Germany also. Some of the best painting of this kind was done at Höchst, a factory established by the Elector of Mainz for making faïence as well as porcelain, and at Kiel. To survey in detail the local developments of faïence in all parts of Germany would not here be possible. From Germany the manufacture spread in 1722 to Copenhagen, and from Denmark it was carried very soon after to Sweden, where factories were established in the immediate neighbourhood of Stockholm, at Rörstrand and Marieberg; the former continued until, in recent times, it was transferred to Gustavsberg (compare p. 121).

Early importations of maiolica from Antwerp into England have already been mentioned. In 1567 we have the first record of Netherlandish potters settling in this country, first at Norwich and three years later in London, and from this period we may date with confidence the beginning of the maiolica craft in England. The earliest tangible evidence, however, is a plate in the London Museum, dated 1601, with a border of crude grotesques in Italian style and an inscription in praise of Queen Elizabeth. Soon after, dated specimens become numerous of what it is customary to call " Lambeth delft ", although the potteries in which they were made were not confined to Lambeth but were spread out down the river into Southwark, and were busily productive well before Delft had won fame as a pottery town.

About 1620 we find wares with parti-coloured leaves obviously traceable to a decoration much favoured by Venetian maiolica painters; soon after, artless imitations appear of the birds in landscapes often to be seen on late Ming blue-and-white export porcelain, either alone or combined with no less unsophisticated plagiarisms of the grotesques on Urbino maiolica, whilst several of the moulded relief designs of Bernard Palissy were copied, but with no attempt at faithfulness in the colouring. The Lambeth wares become more interesting when they develop styles of their own. Amongst the most pleasing are the round-bellied wine-bottles with the name of their contents inscribed in excellent blue lettering on a white enamel of fine quality. From about 1635 polychrome wares with scriptural figure-objects become common, notably the Fall, as well as dishes with standing or equestrian figures of sovereigns from Charles I onwards and other notables, often very crudely rendered. Artistically the greatest success of the Lambeth delft potteries in the seventeenth century are dishes with a symmetrical arrangement of growing tulips and other flowers in bright colours within a border of blue dashes (Plate X, B); though of Dutch derivation (compare p. 93) these floral patterns were developed in England in a distinctive manner, showing an excellent sense of design and colour. Towards the end of the century, as recent researches have made

clear,[1] Chinese designs returned to favour, now reflecting the styles of the K'ang Hsi period, but handled
with a freedom that makes them virtually new compositions, often of admirably decorative quality.

From London the manufacture of delft spread before
1650 to Brislington, near Bristol, to be taken up later
in Bristol itself. The earlier wares show tulip designs
and themes from Ming porcelain similar to those of
the Lambeth wares. About the middle of the eighteenth
century many charming landscape and floral designs
appear in which Chinese and English elements are sometimes amusingly combined in harmonious colouring of
lower tone than that prevalent a century before; a
type in which such painting is done within a border of
flowers in opaque white, on a bluish-grey enamel, is
believed to have been made especially at the pottery
of Joseph Flower. In the eighteenth century Liverpool
and Dublin also had delft factories. Punch-bowls
made to order with careful paintings of ships that
called at the port, are the most striking of the Liverpool
productions; tiles were also made, to be decorated by
the firm of Sadler and Green with transfer prints in
black, red or mauve.

Delft ware with its liability to chip and disclose an
unsightly dark " body " beneath its white enamel was
no match for the more serviceable cream-coloured ware
introduced by Wedgwood. Like maiolica and other
classes of tin-enamelled ware made on the Continent,
it was driven from the market, and its manufacture
barely survived in England into the nineteenth century.
Thus a class of pottery which was rivalled in gaiety of
colour only by porcelain languished and in places
succumbed altogether in competition with the ration-
alized output of modern industry.

[1] See F. H. Garner, " Lambeth earthenware ", in *English Ceramic Circle
Transactions*, 1937, p. 43.

CHAPTER VIII

European Porcelain

CHINESE porcelain first became familiar in Europe in the sixteenth century. As soon as it came to the knowledge of European potters it filled them with the desire to make something like it. Its influence on Italian maiolica has already been referred to (p. 90). There is record of attempts at Venice to master the secret of its composition as early as 1470, but the first experiments of which we have tangible evidence are those set on foot about 1575 by Francis I, Grand Duke of Tuscany. With the help of a Levantine potter he succeeded in producing, in a kiln erected for the purpose in the Boboli Gardens at Florence, a material made up of clay and a glassy frit having the whiteness and translucency of Chinese porcelain but very different in its composition; artificial porcelains of this kind are called "soft paste" in distinction from the hard paste of the true Chinese type. Though suggested by Chinese porcelain, this "Medici porcelain", as it is called, breaks entirely away from the Chinese in its shapes, which are in the Italian early baroque style of the period (Plate XI, A); its decoration, painted in cobalt blue sometimes combined with manganese purple, is as a rule in keeping with this style; sometimes—doubtless owing to the origin of the duke's anonymous assistant—it shows an acquaintance with contemporary Persian wares and the Turkish pottery of Isnik (see p. 67). Direct Chinese influence is not apparent. The production was continued under the Grand Duke's successors, but seems to have come to an end about the baroque metalwork of the period, of angular profile. Casts were also made of the Chinese tea-pots and of Chinese porcelain figures, as well as from European bronzes. Some of the wares were decorated with applied reliefs, of acanthus foliage or else of vine stems and branches of rose with flowers and buds. Attempts to imitate the Chinese under-glaze blue painting were for a long time a failure, but various enamel pigments were used; we find narrow borders in a few spots of various colours, and even very simple landscapes and figure-subjects. These firstlings of the Meissen factory may seem somewhat trivial but in their time they excited enormous interest. It had now been proved that the porcelain brought at such high cost from China could be made at home.

Böttger died young, in 1719. The factory was in danger of collapse, but the situation was saved when the king engaged as its director a painter named Johann Gregor Heroldt, from the rival factory which had already been established at Vienna. Under Heroldt enamel painting was brought to a high degree of perfection; even the difficulties of under-glaze blue painting were mastered. The shapes of the wares were deliberately simplified, largely after Chinese models, in order to provide the amplest possible unbroken surfaces for the enameller. The painted designs were in fact copies of Japanese originals, of which the king had gathered together a large collection for the adornment of his Japanese Palace; the delicate compositions of the Kakiemon school were faithfully imitated, and the floral designs of " Imari ware ", mainly in red, blue and gold (compare p. 81), were adapted or improved upon. Alongside these direct imitations of the Oriental a new and original style of *chinoiseries* was developing, under Heroldt's direction and in part from his own hand, inspired by illustrations, themselves for the most part highly fanciful, in a Dutch book recording an embassy to China. These new decorations exhibit

PLATE XI

A. Cruet, "Medici porcelain",
Florentine
(*Page* 99)

(V. and A. Museum)

B. Porcelain milk-jug, French,
St. Cloud
(*Page* 100)

C. Porcelain plate, German, Meissen (V. and A. Museum)
(*Page* 103)

Chinese engaged in drinking tea, trading, fishing and all sorts of amusing or impossible occupations. Soon it became the custom to enclose these quaint subjects in panels bordered by scrollwork, and to give the figures a landscape setting. From this, about 1730, another step forward led to the substitution of European for Chinese landscapes, with small figures in the foreground, mostly river scenes, of which a few can be recognized as views of Meissen itself or other places in Saxony (Plate XI, c). Another feature, which was to be widely imitated in other countries, was the adoption as early as 1725 of coloured grounds, chiefly canary-yellow, mauve and pale greenish-blue, in which the panels containing the pictorial subjects were reserved; the inspiration for this type of decoration is to be found in the powder-blue Chinese porcelain of the period with reserved panels containing flowers or landscapes in *famille verte* enamels (compare p. 77). Another class of decoration in which Meissen was to point the way for most European factories was polychrome flower-painting. The early flowers of semi-Oriental character known at Meissen as " Indian " were succeeded by naturalistic flowers, called " German " by distinction; at first they were stiffly composed in the manner of botanical illustrations, but about 1735 a freer style supervened which for long dominated porcelain painting all over Europe. During the Seven Years' War (1756–63), in which Saxony was confronted by the rising power of Prussia, Meissen, already beginning to feel the effects of the competition of rivals, lost its supremacy amongst the porcelain-factories of Europe.

After the rudimentary stages the Meissen wares displayed their originality even more in the great variety of their shapes and plastic decoration than in their painting. For this the factory was indebted to the genius of the sculptor, Johann Joachim Kaendler. To Kaendler even more than to Heroldt belongs the credit for creating a true European style in porcelain. He was

summoned to the factory when Augustus the Strong
made demands upon it which its staff found beyond
their powers; the king had conceived the idea of
decorating entirely with porcelain a palace at Dresden
which he called the Japanese Palace. Not only Oriental
porcelain was to be used (compare p. 102) but also wares
from his own royal factory. Its chapel was to have
porcelain fittings (even the organ-pipes were to be of
that material), and a long gallery was to be filled with
figures of birds and animals, some of them life-size,
from studies made in the royal parks and zoological
garden. These great figures, in plain white porcelain
(it was found impossible to devise a muffle-kiln large
enough for firing enamel painting on them), still survive.
Full of vitality though they are, they show by their
cracks and flaws that the talents displayed by Kaendler
as a modeller were being misapplied in a task impossible
of successful execution with the technical resources
then available.

Fortunately for Kaendler, Augustus the Strong died
in 1733 and his son, who succeeded him on the throne,
abandoned his grandiose schemes. The sculptor was
thus set free to devote his extraordinarily fertile imagination and his plastic sense to the creation of works
of art more suited alike to his temperament and to the
material. For about fifteen years he was busily engaged
in modelling for the factory or superintending the work
of others. The new direction for which Kaendler was
responsible is seen notably in the forms chosen for
table wares and vases. In place of Oriental shapes we
find the frank adoption of the Baroque modified to
suit the needs of the material. Plastic decoration was
now to play as important a part as enamelling. Raised
borders in great variety were designed for plates and
dishes; handles and supports were enlivened with
scroll work and foliage. Whole services were designed
in special relief patterns; coffee-pots and tea-pots were
made in the shape of grotesque figures with bird spouts.

Figures were also applied as ornaments on the lids and even on the bodies of vases, and at the same time groups and figures were made in porcelain not only to adorn mantlepieces or as accessories to clocks and other articles of furniture, but also, to comply with a fashion of the day, for the decoration in a striking and amusing manner of the sideboard or tables at state banquets.

It was above all in the immense variety of models for figures, at first baroque in manner and later with rococo scrollwork accessories, that Kaendler displayed his fertility of invention, and this branch of his activity was to inspire to similar production the directors of porcelain-factories in every state of Europe. But it would be impossible here to review the work done in this sphere by Kaendler and his imitators; the space already devoted to Meissen can be justified only by the outstanding importance of the factory in the history not only of pottery but of art in general in the eighteenth century.

The successes achieved under the auspices of Augustus the Strong prompted other princes not only in Germany but all over Europe in due course to imitate his example. In Germany other factories for true, hard-paste porcelain sprang up in quick succession. The earliest, only eight years later than Meissen, was that of Vienna, founded with the help of an enameller who had been on the staff of Böttger; at first a private concern, this factory was in 1744 sold to the Emperor. In its early days Vienna produced table wares of decided merit, with clever use of baroque scrollwork, sometimes painted in black and gold only, in a manner independent of the styles of Meissen. Next in order, but considerably later, came Höchst, the private factory of the Archbishop of Mainz, in which enamel-painted faïence of fine quality was also made (compare p. 96).

About 1750 new foundations follow in quick succession. First came the Bavarian factory, removed

soon after its establishment at Neudeck to Nymphen-
burg, near Munich, and justly graded in the very first
rank for the rococo figure-sculptures of its chief
modeller, Franz Anton Bustelli. Then, within eight
years, followed Berlin, Fürstenberg (the Duke of Brunswick's factory), Frankenthal, under the protection of
the Elector Palatine, and Ludwigsburg, in Württem-
berg. The Berlin factory, begun as a private concern,
was bought in 1763 by Frederick the Great and received
his personal attention; it achieved conspicuous artistic
success with a number of services, tastefully decorated
with rococo scrollwork in relief and gaily painted
flowers, made for the king's use at Potsdam. There
were several other minor factories in Germany, including some in Thuringia which were founded on
commercial lines independently of princely support.

Of the German factories in general, apart from
Meissen and Vienna, it may be said that their title
to a place in the records of pottery is based rather on
their prolific output—mostly of highly individual
character—of porcelain figures than on their table
wares. Most of them were in due course affected by
the influence of Sèvres, and over all, as indeed over
European porcelain in general, there fell a blight when
they were called upon to fit in with the ideas of the
Classical Revival. The sober restraint thereby imposed involved a deliberate renunciation of the gaiety
to the expression of which porcelain with its sparkling
glaze and bright enamels so readily lends itself. Complete stultification came at last when, under the dictates
of Napoleon, porcelain was looked upon chiefly as a
vehicle for the painter's art, and its beauty as a material
was as a rule completely hidden from view under a
smothering load of opaque enamels and gilding.

Whilst most countries were subordinate to the
influence of Meissen, France, already meriting distinction for its early commercial ventures in making
soft-paste porcelain, holds a position of its own through

the prowess of a great national institution, the royal manufacture at Sèvres. It was nevertheless to the success of Meissen that Sèvres owed its origin. At a time when the porcelain industry carried on at St. Cloud, Chantilly and other small factories was being seriously menaced by the thriving export trade from Saxony, two employees dismissed from Chantilly, brothers named Dubois, got into touch with a nobleman, Orry de Fulvy, who was interested in promoting French commercial enterprise; he willingly listened to their proposals for the establishment of a new factory in the hope of discovering the secret of true hard porcelain. As brother of a court official charged with the control of public buildings and manufactures, Orry de Fulvy had no difficulty in securing for the purpose quarters in the keep of the royal castle of Vincennes. The experiments there conducted were at first fruitless, but the sagacity of an associate of the Dubois averted impending failure, and in 1745, after four more years of experiment, a satisfactory material was at last produced.

In that year an exclusive royal privilege for twenty years was obtained, for the manufacture of porcelain *façon de Saxe* (*i.e.* like that of Meissen), *c'est-à-dire peinte et dorée, à figures humaines*. The king himself, Louis XV, whose connexion with Saxony through marriage to a daughter of the Elector Augustus III disposed him to take an interest in porcelain, contributed large sums to the undertaking; it also enjoyed the enthusiastic patronage of Madame de Pompadour. In 1759, when it was on the point of financial collapse, the king acquired the factory as royal property, and through all changing forms of government it has remained ever since a French national establishment

The factory owed its rapid advance to a position of outstanding distinction to the fact that, from its very first organization under royal protection, it was placed in the hands of men who were in the front

rank of their several professions. The technical side of
the work was controlled by the chemist, Jean Hellot.
The court goldsmith Duplessis and the sculptor Etienne
Falconet were appointed chief modellers; designs for
painters and modellers alike were supplied by François
Boucher. In 1756 the manufacture was moved from
Vincennes to the site which it still occupies at Sèvres.

Unlike St. Cloud and Chantilly, Vincennes porcelain
shows only slight traces of Oriental influence. The
productions of the early period are mostly painted with
simple floral designs or landscapes in the Meissen
manner. A surprisingly large proportion of the Vincennes revenue was derived from making artificial
flowers in porcelain, to be mounted on metal stems
as embellishments of ormolu candlesticks and clocks.
With the appointment of a competent staff shortly
after 1750 the factory quickly developed a style of
its own, which soon displaced that of Meissen as the
dominant influence in other European porcelain-works.
Vases were designed by Duplessis and others in entirely
original and sometimes extravagant forms (Plate XII,
A), such as the *vaisseau à mat* (of which there is a famous
example in the Wallace Collection), a vase with
elephant-head handles, and another surmounted by a
fountain between two dolphins. Beside a Chinese jar
of the Sung dynasty, for instance, or a mediæval English pitcher, such inventions may be condemned as
aberrations from the strait path of ceramic propriety;
they cannot be fairly judged unless they are con-
sidered as adjuncts to the architectural splendours of
a royal palace such as Versailles. As such they display
to the full the French genius for monumental composition, whilst in beauty of material and perfection of
workmanship they are hardly surpassed by anything
made in porcelain.

The same sense of design is shown in the forms created
for table services, whilst vases and services alike display
an inexhaustible variety and richness of decoration.

Simple and often charming vignettes of landscape, bird or figure subjects, amongst which cupids in the manner of Boucher often play a part, were from an early stage set in panels reserved on a ground of coloured enamel and enclosed by carefully chased gilding. The idea of a coloured ground was borrowed from Meissen and ultimately from Chinese powder blue (compare p. 78), but Vincennes and Sèvres evolved for the purpose enamels such as the *gros bleu* and *bleu de roi*, *bleu céleste*, *rose Pompadour* and *vert pomme*, of unsurpassed richness, which were to be emulated, mostly with slight success, in other European factories. In the earlier stages form and decoration blend in a combination which, however sumptuous, shows vitality of invention and consistent good taste. From this standard there was a gradual declension when Louis XV had been succeeded by his grandson and Queen Marie Antoinette was the dominant influence. The reserved panels on the coloured grounds were filled with pictures entirely concealing the white surface of the porcelain, instead of the earlier simple vignettes; for less expensive services border-patterns were devised which did not make up by their complexity for the lack of taste shown in their conception. An important development took place on the technical side when the discovery of beds of kaolin near Limoges made possible, in 1770—after lengthy researches, the regular production at Sèvres of hard-paste porcelain. The factory was already in decline when the Revolution in 1793 brought it to the verge of extinction. It was rescued by Napoleon and required to devote itself entirely to the output of hard-paste, for the production of which numerous small factories had been started in Paris and elsewhere in France. The subsequent career of Sèvres belongs to the history of modern times.

In the second half of the eighteenth century few states of Europe were without their porcelain factories, either princely or commercial. At Tournay, in Belgium,

soft-paste porcelain of excellent quality was made
from 1750 onwards; the factory is of interest because
of its staff connexions, as yet incompletely investigated,
with Chelsea. In Italy there were important factories
at Venice, near Florence (at the villa of the Marchese
Ginori at Doccia) and, under the protection of Charles
III, King of Naples (son-in-law of Augustus the Strong
of Saxony), in the precincts of his palace at Capo di
Monte. When Charles succeeded to the throne of
Spain in 1759 he took with him the entire staff of his
Neapolitan factory to establish a new one on similar
lines near Madrid, at Buen Retiro. The Doccia factory
is carried on to the present day as part of a large
Italian combine of ceramic establishments.

England was a late entrant in the field of porcelain
manufacture. The experiments of Dwight in the
seventeenth century (see p. 38) did not achieve the
desired result. Priority belongs to two factories in the
outskirts of London. In 1744 a patent was granted to
Thomas Frye and Edward Heylyn for a factory at Bow,
but it is doubtful whether it began operation until the
following year. A cream-jug in the British Museum with
the inscription *Chelsea* 1745 incised under its base, is
evidence that the famous Chelsea factory had begun
its career at least as early as that date. The metro-
politan factories were followed in quick succession by
others in the provinces founded shortly before or soon
after 1750—Bristol, Worcester (1751), Derby, Longton
Hall in Staffordshire, and Lowestoft. The porcelain
made in all of these was alike in being of the soft-paste
type, but differed as regards the ingredients in its composition. It was not until 1768 that the discovery of
kaolin in Cornwall led to the establishment at Plymouth by William Cookworthy, a chemist resident in
the town, of a factory for making true, hard-paste
porcelain; he was guided in his procedure by the
letters of a French missionary describing the manufacture in China.

PLATE XII

A. Porcelain vase, French, Sèvres
(*Page* 108)

B. Vase, Wedgwood's blue jasper ware
(*Page* 126)

C. Porcelain teapot, Chelsea
(*Page* 111)
(A, C, Victoria and Albert Museum; B, Castle Museum, Nottingham)

Chelsea stands easily first amongst the English factories. In spite of technical defects never completely eliminated, the " bodies " made there, especially about 1755, in what is known from the mark employed as the " red-anchor period ", are of beautiful quality; like that of Sèvres, the soft creamy glaze was a very sympathetic recipient for the enamel pigments, which coalesce with it more readily than those on hard-paste porcelain. Whether in flower-painting or in figure-subjects, the Chelsea enamellers to a large extent imitated foreign types, at first Japanese, then those of Meissen, later of Sèvres, but a certain originality is as a rule shown in handling the borrowed themes. Towards 1760 rich ground-colours were introduced, rivalling those of Sèvres, notably a deep mazarine blue and the so-called claret colour (Plate XII, c). For its shapes Chelsea at first copied for the most part originals in silver, both its first and its second proprietors being silversmiths; it was the latter, Nicolas Sprimont, a native of Liége, who by his enterprise secured for the factory Court and society patronage. Under Sprimont's management Meissen models were to some extent adopted, and porcelain figures in emulation of Meissen but often of original design formed a large proportion of the output. Sumptuous vases and candelabra in a rococo style of their own, richly enamelled and gilt, were also produced. In 1770 financial difficulties led to the purchase of the factory by William Duesbury, who sixteen years before had set up as a china manufacturer at Derby; for some time the two factories were carried on together under his control. During this " Chelsea-Derby " period Duesbury set himself to cater for the fashionable world by revolutionizing the style of decoration in conformity with the new classical standards of the day, already adopted for his wares by Josiah Wedgwood (see p. 44); the riotous rococo of late Chelsea gave way to striped patterns and simple sprigs in restrained colouring applied to shapes of

corresponding sobriety. The decoration adopted for
table services at Derby in the last decades of the
eighteenth century is almost unsurpassed in its suit-
ability alike for the material and for the intended
purpose of the ware. Landscape-painting reflecting
an English enthusiasm of the time was much employed, with a good judgment in adaptation to the
medium lacking in later developments, when it continued in favour for decorating the tasteless productions of the factory in its last stages (it closed down
in 1848).

The decoration of Bow porcelain in its earlier years
followed the Oriental manner indicated by the title,
" New Canton ", adopted for the factory; this phase
was succeeded by artless imitations of Meissen and
Chelsea. Technically Bow porcelain is of interest as the
first in which bone-ash was used as an ingredient,
afterwards to be adopted in the standard English china
" body ". Lowestoft china is akin to Bow, but even
humbler in its pretensions; it is in consequence æsthetically less unstable. The proprietors were satisfied with
catering for the needs of such clients as its neighbourhood provided.

The Worcester factory, still carried on, though not
on its original site, was, in some way as yet not fully
ascertained, connected with a short-lived porcelain
manufacture conducted in a glass-house at Bristol.
From this its proprietors seem to have acquired the
secret of using soapstone (steatite) as an ingredient.
The " body " thus composed seems to have been more
manageable than those employed at Chelsea and elsewhere. The factory was started on sound business
lines; its wares were intended primarily to be serviceable and are from the first remarkable for their sound
technical qualities. The decoration is as a rule simple
and unaffected, following, but not slavishly copying, at
first Oriental and later Continental models (Plate V, B).
Here also some attempt was made to emulate the rich

ground-colours of Sèvres; the "scale blue"—overlapping scale-pattern painted in a soft dark underglaze blue—was especially popular. Worcester was the first porcelain-factory to adopt transfer-printing, introduced a short time before in the enamel-works at Battersea, as an easy and therefore inexpensive method of decoration. The prints, from copper plates skilfully engraved, were at first executed in black and other enamel colours; printing in under-glaze blue was a later development, much employed also at a small neighbouring porcelain-factory at Caughley, in Shropshire.

The factory founded in 1768 at Plymouth was transferred in 1770 to Bristol, where it continued for about thirteen years to produce hard-paste porcelain with decoration in a pleasant but unimaginative style conforming to the taste of the period. The concern was afterwards acquired by a Staffordshire company which, at New Hall, Shelton, produced wares worthy to be commended for their appropriate if unassuming decoration.

CHAPTER IX

Modern Times

IN the modern period since the beginning of the nineteenth century the art of the potter has in general declined, under the stress of growing industrialism. In peasant workshops, alike in China and Japan and in Europe, including England, as well as amongst savage tribes in America and Africa, sound craftsmanship was still kept up and in remote places continues even to the present day, but with dwindling vitality. Apart from such spheres pottery tends to fall into two classes—useful wares turned out on lines of mass production, and ornamental vases made by individual potters whose initial training has been that normal in the modern school of art; there is also a large body of wares intended to be decorative but so entirely lacking in artistic quality that they are not worth serious consideration. Of useful pots, made largely by machinery, mathematical precision and uniformity of shape and size are required, to fit them for taking their place amongst other mechanically made appliances; the result is that such æsthetic merits as it is possible for them to possess are those of a well-constructed machine, limited to the satisfaction given by a thing well fitted to do its job (only in colour, and not always even there, can there be some latitude beyond these limits). Decorative wares depend more than formerly upon the personality of the artist-potter; they are of interest only if their maker or designer is a man or woman of strong character, able to assert individuality against the handicaps imposed by the well-intended, but too often misguided curriculums of academic instruction. Changes of style there have been, in both classes of production, but changes imposed by arbitrary enthusiasms for ancient models, not brought about spontaneously under the stimulus of altered conditions of life. Artistic invention has stagnated and recourse has been had in its default to plagiarism. Only in quite recent times has there been emancipation from the disastrous effects of nineteenth-century thraldom to the styles of the past.

It would be impossible and hardly interesting to follow the course taken, even by the leading factories only, in the various European countries during the first half of the nineteenth century. In many of them the manufacture of porcelain was combined with that of several types of earthenware or fine stoneware. Under the auspices of Napoleon the Empire style, elaborated from Ancient Egyptian and Roman models, was introduced at Sèvres. Its extravagances as there practised set the fashion for royal and even commercial factories in most countries of Europe. England, partly no doubt as a result of her unconquered isolation, held to a large extent aloof from this movement.

The opportunities afforded by troubles in France to British society from the Prince Regent downwards of collecting on easy terms the splendid Sèvres porcelain of the *ancien régime* resulted as early as the second decade of the century in attempts to imitate it; the small short-lived porcelain-factories carried on at this time in South Wales, at Swansea and Nantgarw, produced various types of glassy soft porcelain of excellent quality with decorations inspired or even literally copied from Sèvres of the time of Louis XV. In other factories, such as those of Worcester and some in Staffordshire, provision was made for the revived fashion for *chinoiserie* seen in its most extravagant form in the architecture of the Pavilion at Brighton;

the wares made under this impulse are for the most part
clumsy in shape and, in their over-loaded decoration,
entirely lacking in the charm and individuality which
most eighteenth-century European porcelain in Oriental
style has to recommend it. A vulgar excess of harsh
colours and gilding is the mark of most porcelain made
in England for several decades from about 1810 onwards; the productions of the Rockingham factory,
at Swinton in Yorkshire, and the contemporary wares
of Derby are the worst offenders. A word of approval,
on the other hand, may be bestowed on some of the
table services made soon after 1800 in Staffordshire.
Here the New Hall works (see p. 113) and the lately
founded Minton factory at Stoke-on-Trent produced
porcelain displaying a number of simple border designs
as appropriate as they are original; some are faintly
reminiscent of chintz patterns, in others shells and seaweed as well as flowers play a part. The firms of Minton
and Spode also made good use of transfer prints in
stipple, mostly of the landscape subjects popular at the
time, in a quiet tone of grey-black.

The depths of chaos in conflicting styles were reached
when the Great Exhibition of 1851 incited competitors
from all countries to surpass one another in the misguided excesses of their efforts. Bloated perversions of
the Antique, the Gothic, the Rococo, and the Oriental,
all alike showing an entire lack of appreciation of the
true possibilities of the materials employed, jostled
one another in the hope of engaging by their wealth
of decoration the attention of the public. Reaction
came at last.

Emancipation was gradual, in the second half of the
century, along the twofold lines indicated at the beginning of this chapter. Artists trained in the state and
municipal schools of art which had been founded in
most countries, began to turn their attention to pottery
as well as other forms of " applied art "; the direction
taken by them was at first suggested by the specimens

of ancient craftsmanship exhibited in the museums then also newly established. Something parallel to the work of Kenzan and other artist potters of Japan (see p. 80) was the result; individuals followed their own predilections with little attention to social requirements and only very slight influence on industrial design. More effective were the decorative wares produced in the various state factories such as Meissen, Sèvres and Copenhagen.

In official quarters the lead was given by Sèvres. Amongst several technical innovations started at that factory was the development of porcelain slip decoration in what is known as *pâte sur pâte*; cameo reliefs were applied in white over a superficial layer stained black, grey or celadon-green not by means of moulds as in the case of Wedgwood's jasper ware, but freehand, in soft slip, with the help of modelling tools and a wet brush. This process, introduced about 1860, was exploited most successfully and in a highly personal style of figure composition by M. L. Solon, who, in 1870, quitted Sèvres and obtained a post in the Minton factory at Stoke-on-Trent which he retained till the beginning of the present century. An artist who worked about the same time at Sèvres after previous employment at Minton's was the sculptor Albert Carrier-Belleuse. At Sèvres the *pâte sur pâte* method was taken up by Taxile Doat, sometimes in combination with a high-temperature crimson glaze imitating the Chinese *sang-de-bœuf*. The extension in range of high-temperature coloured glazes and pigments was a notable success of the Sèvres factory towards the end of the nineteenth century. It may be noted that at this period the sculptor Émile Rodin was, for a short time, in its employ.

The opening up of contact with Japan resulted in an enthusiasm for Japanese craftsmanship which was not without effect on pottery manufacture in Europe. One of its less fortunate results is seen in the porcelain produced at Worcester in the 1870's with laboriously cut openwork ornament or made to simulate in outward appearance Japanese work in other materials such as ivory and lacquer. The only wholesome fruit of this contact was the movement set on foot in 1884 at Copenhagen, when the royal Danish factory was reorganized and Arnold Krog was put in charge of its artistic development. Krog turned his attention to the designing of shapes more in accordance with the spirit of the material than had for long prevailed in Europe; for decoration he adopted, instead of the customary enamel colours, under-glaze pigments capable of resisting the very high temperature which a new type of hard porcelain then introduced at the factory required for its firing. The motives chosen by Krog and his assistants, painted in soft blue alone or in combination with green, grey and mauve, show Japanese influence in their treatment but were of entirely local derivation; the artists favoured the flowers and wild life and, most of all, the landscape of their native Denmark. Side by side with useful wares and vases a large number of figures illustrating the rural life of the country, human and animal, were produced from models by able sculptors. About 1900 scientific research led to the invention of crystalline glazes, and in the period since the war attention has been paid to other high-temperature glazes, sometimes aided in their development by their application to a porcellanous stoneware "body" in emulation of mediæval Chinese wares. In these materials remarkable figures as well as vases and bowls with vigorously engraved figure-subjects have lately been made by Jais Nielsen.

The technique of high-temperature glazes and painting was taken over from Copenhagen by other porcelain factories, notably Berlin and Meissen. In France attention was usefully turned to work in colour-glazed stoneware, again under Japanese or Chinese influence. At the end of the nineteenth century, good work in

PLATE XIII

A. Stoneware water-pot, Japanese, Seto, "Shino ware"
(*Page* 80)

B. Stoneware tea-bowl, made by Kenzan, Japanese
(*Page* 80)

C. Stoneware bowl, made by William Staite Murray
(*Page* 120)

(All, Victoria and Albert Museum)

PART II — GLASS

CHAPTER I

Glass in Antiquity

GLASS is a material which, in modern times, has attained an importance hardly surpassed by that of any other product of human inventiveness. In scientific research, in architecture and engineering, as an aid to sight, and for countless purposes of household life it plays an indispensable part in civilization. Yet this vast expansion of its function has come about in a period of little more than two centuries, which is short in comparison with the great antiquity of the material itself, and does not concern us in the present work. We have here to consider the history and development of glass as the material of articles which, though mostly designed for a useful purpose, deserve by reason of their beauty to be regarded also as works of art.

Although glass is of great antiquity, in the form in which it is usually thought of it is much less ancient than pottery and several other kinds of artifact. When we talk of glass we have in mind chiefly glass vessels and windows; the small articles such as beads and other kinds of jewellery in the making of which glass first made its appearance, are of small account and much less important nowadays than they were in antiquity. Windows, and the superb art of the glass-painter born in mediæval Europe out of their invention, would require a treatise to themselves and are accordingly omitted from our consideration. We shall therefore confine ourselves to vessels made of glass, leaving out of account also various other articles known in modern speech by the word "glass", in the singular or plural, without further qualification. Glass in the form of vessels was little made before the invention of the blowing-iron, which took place less than two thousand years ago; when once this implement had been invented the glass-maker's craft grew rapidly, and glass as we commonly think of it to-day became a customary adjunct of civilized life.

Glass and pottery have something in common. Mineral substances are essential constituents of both, and both require heat in their production; they are amongst what the French call *les arts du feu*; but they present obvious and striking differences. Whilst both can be given their shape and most of their decoration only when they are in a soft condition, this state in the one case is the result of firing, in the other precedes it. Glass only comes into being when its materials have been fused together by heat, and can be worked with any facility only when it has been molten by fire into a soft condition; pottery, also worked when the materials are soft and plastic, goes to the kiln after, not before, being shaped. Glass is hardened by cooling, pottery by heating. Most glass vessels are shaped by expansion from within outwards by the breath of the glass-blower; pots are formed under inward pressure from the hand of the thrower as the clay turns on the wheel (though other methods are in use this is the primary and, through the ages, the commonest process).

Glass is a composite material made by fusing together various substances of which the essentials are silica and an alkali in combination with lime or lead. The silica is usually in the form of sand, but powdered calcined flints can also be employed; for the alkali use has been made at various times in the past of potash, obtained by burning wood, especially beechwood, or fern, or of soda from the ashes of seaweed. Lead, although not unknown in the glass of the ancient world, was not commonly used until, as will presently be related, it became the distinctive ingredient of the so-called " flint glass " of modern times. Almost from the beginnings of the art it was known that glass could be coloured by the inclusion in its composition of various minerals. The presence of iron as an impurity in the ingredients is the cause of a greenish or yellowish brown tone in much glass made by primitive methods; to counteract such discoloration various bleaching agents can be employed such as manganese. The principal staining materials used in ancient times were copper to produce light blue, green and blood red, cobalt for dark blue, manganese for amethyst-colour or brownish purple, antimony for yellow, and iron for various hues from green, as in ordinary bottle-glass, to brown and black. An opaque white is obtainable from tin, and tin can be used as an opacifying agent with other colouring materials, but in some cases the opacity of glass is due not to tin but to the presence in it of a dense multitude of minute enclosed bubbles.

The properties which give to glass its distinctive aptitude for artistic manipulation are its cohesiveness and its extreme ductility when in a viscous condition, in the stage of cooling from the molten state. When gathered up on the iron from the melting-pot glass can be blown into a bubble of extreme tenuity or drawn out into the finest of threads; it can be twisted into a plaited cord or rolled out into a slab or pinched into a frill. By means of colouring oxides mixed in the molten batch it can be stained with hues hardly surpassed by the most beautiful of natural forms; the names by which the colours of glass have from early times been known—sapphire, amethyst and emerald— imply a comparison which is not unapt. Its translucency makes it the most ethereal of artificial substances; by

its reflecting and refracting power it makes of light
itself a wonderful medium for artistic design, and this
quality can be brought into full play by means of
cutting and engraving tools when the material, suitably
compounded, has been reduced by cooling to a hard
condition.

When once the use of the blowing-iron had been
discovered these multifarious properties of glass could
be and soon were exploited to the full; but as we shall
see, this discovery came relatively late in the history
of civilization, much later, for instance, than the invention of the potter's wheel or the working of metallic
ores. The earliest blown glass vessels date from the
first century before Christ at the earliest; before that
time the possible uses of glass were limited in the extreme. The secret of its manufacture was already known
in Egypt more than 3000 years before Christ, but then
only as a material for making small articles of jewellery
such as beads and pendants for stringing together as
necklaces or breast ornaments, amulets, rings and
scarabs; the glass paste in its molten state could easily
be moulded or manipulated into a great variety of shapes
sometimes in miniature imitation of flowers or fruit or
as tiny representations of human and other living
creatures. These are often of exquisite beauty and
refinement as miniature works of art. The employment of glass paste for making hollow vessels began
much later; such things make their appearance some
sixteen centuries before Christ, but the Egyptians in
these early times were hindered in the application of
the substance by the limitations of their technique.
Tombs of the Eighteenth Dynasty (about 1500–1350
B.C.) have yielded not only ornaments such as were
being made from earlier times but also useful articles
—small bottles or phials for unguents and perfumes,
made in opaque light- or dark-blue glass paste; any
considerable size was precluded by technical difficulties;
the vessel had to be given its shape by wrapping or

winding the viscous material round a core modelled in clay by hand to the required form and scraped away from the interior when the glass had cooled and hardened. Decoration is nearly always present, in the form of closely set transverse stripes differing in colour from the ground; these were made by pressing fine parallel threads of glass into the surface of the vessel, whilst still in a soft condition; they were as a rule worked into zigzag or feather patterns in exactly the same manner as the combed patterns on the Staffordshire slip ware described on p. 33. Small vessels of this kind continued to be made by the same process and with little change in their general character until Ancient Egypt as an independent state came to an end; new shapes were introduced and a wider range of colours, but the earliest examples were never surpassed either in quality of material or in beauty of colour.

At some date not established with certainty but probably in the reign of the Emperor Augustus the first and greatest revolution in glass manufacture took place; the blowing-iron, already referred to, was invented—a blowpipe by means of which a molten lump of glass could be expanded by the breath of the workman into a bubble. Hollow vessels of a size unknown before now became possible, and it was quickly discovered that they could be made in a great variety of shapes. This invention was of even greater moment to the glass-maker than that of the wheel to the potter, and down to quite recent times no more revolutionary change has occurred in the history of the craft. From that time almost to the present glass technique has continued essentially unaltered; the word " manufacture " has been applicable to it in a literal sense. Mechanical power has come on the scene so lately that less than a generation ago a glasshouse with a large output was being carried on in the heart of London on lines differing hardly at all in many respects from those obtaining in the Middle Ages; even a Roman

glass-blower would have found there little to puzzle
him in the materials or tools employed, nor would the
articles made have seemed greatly beyond his powers.

Early Egyptian glass was traded all over the then
civilized world and even beyond; the small " core-
wound " phials are found in Crete and Greece, and
beads were carried as far as Britain and the Baltic
and into the heart of Africa. When the power of Rome
was extended over the whole of southern and western
Europe, glass manufacture spread from its original
home in Egypt and on the coast of Palestine and Syria
almost to the farthest limits of the Empire.   Glasshouses were set up not only in Italy but also in Spain,
Northern Gaul, Britain, and what is now Germany. An
important centre was in Campania, and in the second
and third centuries after Christ Cologne also became
a seat of the manufacture from which glass of fine
quality was distributed throughout the neighbouring
regions and over the sea to Britain; there was a flourishing glass industry also in Picardy. This geographical
expansion was matched by technical developments no
less surprising, and it is almost true to say that the
glass-blowers of the Roman world were acquainted with
all the processes known to their successors until the
quite recent invasion of the industry by mechanical
power; certainly they have never been surpassed in
technical skill and æsthetic sensibility, even if they were
obliged to achieve with much labour what, owing to
mechanical aids, can now be done with a much smaller
expenditure of human energy.

Anything like a complete survey of Ancient Roman
glass would be impossible within the limits of this book;
only the more significant types can be referred to.
With the introduction of the blowing-iron transparent
glass first began to be made.   The earliest Roman
glass was of the type in which the alkali employed is
soda; it was composed essentially of silica, soda and
lime.   Coloured glass was made, as in earlier ages in

Egypt, by adding to these substances the various staining oxides to which reference has already been made,
but of the vast quantities of glass that have come
down to us from the first few centuries after Christ the
greater part has no colour other than that due to impurities in the sand employed; a certain iron content
is almost always present, and to this is due the green
tone of greater or less intensity which is characteristic
of the commonest kinds of transparent glass, not only
of the Roman period. It was quickly discovered that
this greenish tone could be counteracted by adding a
small proportion of manganese to the composition, and
some Roman glass is almost colourless.

A sound judgment of the capabilities of the material
is almost invariably shown even in vessels made in
common bluish-green glass for the most ordinary uses
and entirely devoid of ornament; there is æsthetic satisfaction to be found in the small phials, bottles, cups
and bowls dug up all over the territories of the Roman
empire, or the globular cinerary urns with conical lid
and the large cylindrical or square wine-jars, with
corrugated handles which have been likened to celery-
stalks, found in graves of the first and second centuries.
The last-mentioned vessels are evidence of the use of
moulds for giving shapes other than circular to the
expanding bubble of "metal" (as it is called by the
glass-maker) on the blowing-iron. The same con-
trivance was used for obtaining patterns in relief. The
earliest relief-moulded glasses are small bottles with
Medusa heads, rosettes, and other ornaments, made
probably at Sidon; to judge from the Greek inscriptions
moulded on some of them they are the work of Greek
or Hellenized artisans, of whom a certain Ennion
seems to have been one of the most prolific, with a
large overseas trade. Moulded signatures are found at
a later date on ordinary useful wares made, probably
at Boulogne-sur-Mer, by Gaulish glass-blowers such as
Frontinus, the name of whose workshop often occurs

under the base of cylindrical jars with horizontal reeding
like the hoops of a barrel.

Far more interesting and attractive is the decoration
produced by manipulation of the "metal" in its
viscous state with the help of tongs and other tools.
The bubble itself could be pinched or pushed into a
diversity of shapes, or "metal" drawn out into threads
could be wound round it or applied so as to form zigzag
or network patterns, or buttons could be stuck on and
impressed with small moulds to form lions' masks,
rosettes and other relief ornaments. Again, spots or

Fig. 13a, b.—Two Roman cups (Victoria and Albert Museum)

embossments could be dropped on to the surface in
"metal" stained in the wide range of colouring which
already in Roman times was available to the glass-
maker; some of the loveliest Roman glasses are the
bowls and beakers in shapes of simple dignity to which
interest has been added by studding the surface with a
few spots of blue, green or purple placed with unfailing
æsthetic judgment (fig. 13b). Staining of the entire
substance is also the chief beauty of much Roman
glass; this is true conspicuously of certain saucers in
the form almost of a shallow segment of a globe, without a foot-ring, and slender beakers rising with a slight
convexity from a small foot, which were amongst the
products especially of Alexandrian glasshouses of the
first century after Christ. Objects of this class some-

times have simple decoration done by a technique anticipating that of the German glasshouses of the seventeenth century and their imitators, namely, engraving on the wheel; a band round the edge of a saucer, or a horizontal line or two breaking up into well-proportioned zones the elevation of a goblet (fig. 13*a*), serve to enhance their austere beauty of shape. We have here an important new development in that the work can only be done when the " metal " has been reduced by cooling to a hard condition. The same technique—that of the gem-engraver—was used with astounding skill to grind out of a solid mass of coloured glass vessels of highly complicated form; by this laborious process were fashioned cups with high foot and two ring-handles reproducing a shape first made in silver, as exemplified in the treasures discovered at Hildesheim and Boscoreale.

It is perhaps in the sphere of colour that the glass of classical antiquity surpasses the achievements of any later period; only in the windows of mediæval cathedrals has equal glory of colour been attained. Not only were vessels made of a single colour but a great variety of polychrome decoration was produced by elaborating Ancient Egyptian processes. We have seen how the core-wound flasks of the Eighteenth Dynasty were decorated with inlaid stripes by heating and pressing into the surface glass threads of various colours. A new development was now introduced; canes and rods of different colours were fused together in bundles (sometimes spirally twisted), and then sections were cut at right angles or slantways to the direction of the rods; by embedding in a sheath of colourless glass a number of such rods or segments assembled inside a hollow mould, it became possible to produce saucers and bowls veined in imitation of agate or other semi-precious stones, or those studded with variegated stars and rosettes of the type to which, in modern times, the Italian name of *millefiori* has been applied. Another

kind of mosaic glass was made by embedding on the
surface of the heated bubble chips and shreds of various
coloured glass in kaleidoscopically fortuitous arrangement. These products of Alexandrian and Italian glasshouses of the Augustan age were treasured as works of
art by Roman citizens even in a time when glass must
have been as common in their houses as fine porcelain
is in the modern world.

It may be mentioned here that the brilliant iridescence often found on ancient glass, particularly on the
commonest kinds of transparent greenish glass, was
not intended by their makers but is the result of decom-
position of the " metal " through burial; where suitable conditions exist these rainbow hues will form
themselves on certain kinds of modern glass after no
long period of interment.

A high degree of skill was called for by another difficult process introduced at Alexandria in the same
period. This was the production of a design in two
colours by coating a vessel with an outer layer of a
different colour and then partially grinding away this
layer on the engraver's wheel; the coating was obtained
by dipping the vessel into glass of the desired colour in
a molten state. The result of the two proceedings when
finished was a vessel of one colour with relief ornament
of another. The most famous and most important
known example of this technique, which must have
been difficult and costly, is the Portland Vase, found
in a marble sarcophagus of the third century under
a tumulus opened by command of Pope Urban VIII
(Maffeo Barberini); its classical designs, in white
cameo relief on a blackish-blue ground, are familiar
from the copies made in pottery by Josiah Wedgwood
(see p. 46) and countless imitators. Fragments dug
up in Egypt prove that reliefs in more than one colour
were sometimes applied to a single vessel. The wheel
was also employed for simple linear decoration, as
already mentioned, and for faceted and honeycomb

patterns similar to those of modern cut glass; figure subjects were also sometimes cut in intaglio or more often rendered by line engraving. Such cut and engraved glass was made especially in the Rhineland, at Cologne and Treves, in the third century; the discovery of a cutting-wheel of stone together with fragments of facet-cut vessels on the site of a Roman glasshouse at Wilderspool in South Lancashire proves that the technique was practised in Britain as well. To the Cologne region belong also the extraordinary *tours de force* in the shape of goblets with inscriptions and other designs forming a network standing free, and attached to the surface of a cup or bowl only by a few connecting struts.   Another anticipation of later technique was in the use of designs, including figure-subjects, painted on the surface in enamel colours— pigments, that is to say, consisting of coloured glass ground into a powder and mixed with an oily medium; a fragment of enamelled glass has been found on the farthest confines of the Empire in one of the forts on the Roman Wall in Northumberland.

It remains to mention another kind of Ancient Roman glass, which is significant not only for its technique but also for its great importance as a sidelight on the early history of Christianity. In the catacombs of Rome have been found, affixed to the sepulchral recesses, large numbers of small glass disks with designs scratched through gold leaf embedded in the substance of the metal; they originally filled the bottoms of cups or bowls, or were dispersed over their sides. The engraved subjects on some of the earlier examples, dating perhaps from the second century, are mythological, but in the great majority of cases, like the fresco paintings on the vaults of the catacombs, they relate to Christian symbolism or Bible history and have a bearing on the development of Christian dogma. Some of the finest engravings, from about the end of the fourth century, are portraits carried out in minute detail; a first-rate example may be seen at South Kensington. The technique doubtless originated at Alexandria, but most of these glasses have been found, and were almost certainly made, in Rome.

CHAPTER II

Decline and Revival

BOTH in the East and in the West Roman traditions of glass-making survived to form the basis of the far less skilful craftsmanship of the Middle Ages, although many centuries were to pass by before any approach was made to Roman glass either in quality of material or in variety of technique; in fact, glass ceased for a time to be the material of vessels for luxurious uses, its place being taken by precious metals or bronze. In the Syrian coast-region the manifold forms of decoration obtainable with the pincers continued in favour down to the Islamic period. In Europe the Rhineland took the lead in glass craftsmanship, which seems to have been introduced there by Levantine immigrants. Here also pincered applied ornaments were employed with good effect. Some forms of great beauty made their appearance in the north-west of the Empire already in the second century; notable amongst them are jugs with a flat-based conical body, often decorated with well-spaced and delicate ribbing either vertical or spiral, long tubular neck divided by a slight constriction from the body, and strap handle strengthened by a spine applied along its length, drawn downwards into a long spur giving strong attachment to the body and often notched into a comb. A jug in the British Museum, found at Barnwell near Cambridge, and another of deep yellowish-olive tone in the Royal Museum, Canterbury (Plate XIV, B), may be cited as examples of outstanding distinction. Both Frankish and Anglo-Saxon graves of

the sixth and seventh century, the period of the first
Teutonic settlements in England, have yielded quantities of vessels which show that although the quality
of the metal is not equal to that of the great age of
Rome, the principles of glass technique continued to
be well understood. Some shapes of drinking-glass
peculiar to the Teutonic world make their appearance
at this time. Strangest of these is the small-based
conical beaker decorated with rows of hollow excres-
cences shaped like an elephant's trunk. Another characteristic form is the round-based waisted tumbler
made to stand only when inverted and intended to be
emptied of its contents at a single draught; the same
is the intention of the glass imitations, often elabor-
ately ornamented in relief with transverse bands and
zigzags, of that essentially northern utensil the drink-
ing-horn, and of the footless beakers of narrow tapering
shape, sometimes decorated with fine threads applied
lengthways as ribs or elongated scallops, which are
amongst the loveliest of all things made in glass.
From these products of the Dark Ages the German
glasses of the mediæval period were the natural descendants.

Revival in the art first came, however, not in Europe
but in its earliest home, in the East. After the faith of
Islam had spread victorious over a large part of the
Mediterranean, Egypt under its Fatimite rulers in the
tenth and eleventh centuries was brought once more
to a high degree of civilized culture. Alexandria again
became a centre of the production of fine glass, but
glass-making seems to have been widespread over the
Islamic world; not only in Egypt and Syria but also
in Mesopotamia and Persia excavations have yielded
glasses, and of more than one variety, which although
hardly distinguishable appear to be of local origin. As
in Europe in later times so in the Near East glass-
blowers wandered from land to land carrying with
them their technical secrets, so that it is rarely possible

to classify their wares on geographical lines. Common
to most of them is a relatively poor quality of metal,
full of bubbles and seldom free from a pronounced
colour, either greenish or of a pale amber tone, due to
impurities in the materials used.

Amongst the earliest Near-Eastern glass of interest
are small bowls, cups and other vessels with small
ornaments stamped on applied pads—mostly " prunts "
like a raspberry, less often Arabic inscriptions, animals
or birds; technically akin to these are bowls, in which
similar motives are produced in sunk outline by pinching
with tongs like a wafering-iron on each arm of which
the same design stands out in relief.   On a higher
plane altogether are the glasses with wheel-cut decoration. Glyptic art was brought to an unsurpassed degree
of refinement at Alexandria in the tenth and eleventh
centuries; a rock crystal ewer in the Victoria and
Albert Museum, with reliefs of gazelles attacked by
eagles, and another in St. Mark's, Venice, with designs
of the same order, which was amongst the treasures
brought from Constantinople, are well-known examples
of this splendid art. From crystal-cutting the technique
was transferred, as in Roman times, to glass and was
practised especially at Alexandria, although there is
reason to think it was not confined to Egypt.   The
glass objects with wheel-cut decoration are of every
degree of elaboration; from tiny phials about an inch
high cut square and faceted, and long-necked bottles
of austere beauty with decoration limited to one or
two horizontal grooves in the neck and a row of discs
(fig. 14) or pine-cone motives round the body, they
range to imitations of the crystal ewers mentioned
above, as proved by an example, sadly shattered, in the
Buckley Gift at South Kensington; to this surpass-
ingly skilful piece of work no parallel has hitherto been
recorded. The name " Hedwig glasses " has been given
to a number of heavy glass beakers, of the eleventh or
twelfth century, shaped like a modern tumbler, with

volutes and stylized lions or eagles cut in strong relief,
which have been preserved in cathedral treasuries in
Europe; some of them were traditionally associated
with St. Hedwig of Silesia, who is said to have used
them for the miracle of changing water into wine.

In coloured glass also the achievements of Roman

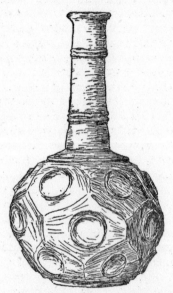

Fig. 14.—Egyptian (Fatimite) cut-glass bottle
(Victoria and Albert Museum)

times were equalled if not surpassed in the late mediæval
glasshouses of Syria and Egypt. The ancient Egyptian
technique of inlaying zigzag bands was revived, but
never with great success. It was in painting that the
Islamic glass-makers excelled, and in decoration of this
kind an entirely new technique was introduced, in
Egypt; painting in lustre colours similar to that on
the earthenware of the period (see p. 63) was, under
the Fatimite rulers and perhaps earlier, practised also

PLATE XIV

A. Glass lamp, Syrian
(Victoria and Albert Museum)
(*Page* 139)

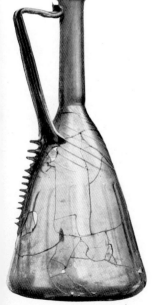

B. Glass jug, Ancient Roman (Royal
Museum, Canterbury)
(*Page* 135)

on glass. Metallic pigments producing when fired a
golden iridescence were used on white or coloured
glass for Arabic inscriptions, floral and animal designs
analogous to those on the pottery. Rare examples
exist also of glass painted with gold itself, in the
manner of the early Christian gilt glasses; a fragmentary bottle in the British Museum, attributed to the
twelfth century, has decoration finely executed in
gilding, with details scratched away with a needle-
point, consisting of dancing girls amongst trees and
eagles, in zones separated by an Arabic inscription
giving titles believed to be those of one of the Atabeks
of Mesopotamia.

The great glory of the craft in the Mohammedan
east was, however, the revival of painting in enamel
colours which, as we have seen, had been practised in
Roman times. The most famous examples of enamelled
glass of this period are the lamps made for lighting
mosques, especially in Cairo, of which the Victoria and
Albert Museum possesses a collection unsurpassed in
Europe (Plate XIV, A). They are of a more or less
stereotyped shape, of bulbous form, contracting to the
spring of a wide flaring neck, and supported either on
a high conical foot or on a low convex ring. A usual
appurtenance of the mosque-lamp was an egg-shaped
ornament with a hole at each end, made as an embellishment of the chain on which the lamp was hung and
enamelled in the same style as the lamp itself. Suitable
inscriptions from the Koran or titles of the Sultans or
other persons by whom the lamps were given to the
mosque are usually the chief feature of the design, and
from these inscriptions they can often be approxi-
mately dated. The earliest on record shows that the
lamp which bears it was made for a mausoleum in
Cairo erected in 1285–6; by the end of the fourteenth
century the art of glass-enamelling in the Near East
was in full decline. Comparison with Persian and
Syrian pottery justifies a date early in the thirteenth

century for certain lamps sparingly painted in several
colours with tiny scattered figures of horsemen, birds or
fishes and slight borders of cresting. The normal type
of design on the later lamps consists of friezes of inscription, in characters of majestic proportions backed
by flowing scrollwork with arabesque foliage and
sometimes interrupted at intervals by medallions containing flowers or heraldic shields. In the period of
decline after the invasions of Mesopotamia and Syria
by the Mongols under Hulagu Khan in 1358, Chinese
influence proclaims itself by the introduction in the
design of phœnixes and Buddhist lotus-flowers, and
inscriptions are sometimes entirely displaced by an
all-over pattern of flowers and foliage; the rich polychrome enamels and gilding of the earlier lamps tend
to become restricted to red, used, as from the beginning, for drawing the outlines, and blue for the background.

Although mosque-lamps are the most conspicuous,
they are by no means the only form of vessel decorated
in this manner. The art is displayed with no less
splendour in two-handled flasks, ewers and bottles
with long slender neck, and amongst the loveliest of
all recipients for it are beakers, generally tubular in
the lower part and conical above. Some of the earliest
of these beakers, dating from the thirteenth century,
are shown by their decoration to have been made for
Christian use and have been preserved in the treasures
of Western churches, to which doubtless they were
given by returning Crusaders. In the British Museum
are two splendid examples, one showing the Virgin
and Child enthroned between St. Peter and St. Paul,
the other with three German shields of arms and the
signature apparently of an Italian artist working in
the Levant. Another exceptional piece of the same
period is a fragmentary dish in the Historisches Museum
at Basle on which is painted the Holy Roman Emperor
enthroned, orb in hand. But of all the many glasses

brought from the East and carefully treasured in Europe, often in costly gold or silver-gilt mounting, none is more famous than the beaker known by its romantic name of the Luck of Edenhall and until recently kept in the ancestral Westmoreland home of the Musgrave family. It is painted in blue, red, green, white and gold with a rich symmetrical pattern of interlaced arabesques of great beauty; it owes its wonderful state of preservation to the case of richly stamped leather made to contain it, probably in England, about the end of the fourteenth century. Where these various types of enamelled glass were made is a question to which no certain answer has hitherto been found. It was at one time supposed that the numerous lamps formerly to be seen in the mosques of Cairo must have been made in Egypt, but all available evidence points to the conclusion that they were imported from abroad and that in Syria, and particularly in the cities of Aleppo and Damascus, the home of this wonderful revival of the art of painted glass is to be sought.

Mention may be made here of the only other development of the craft in the Near East which is of any interest. In the seventeenth and eighteenth centuries glass was made in Persia in distinctive shapes which though very restricted in range are of great beauty; chief amongst them are ewers with long curved spout, and bottles for sprinkling rosewater, bulbous in form and often spirally reeded, with slender sinuous neck ending in an orifice somewhat resembling in shape the flower of an arum lily. The " metal " is sometimes colourless, but more often stained to pleasant tones of blue, amber and violet. A rare type perhaps made or decorated by Persian craftsmen at the court of the Moghul emperors in India, has rich gilt design of flowers and cone-pattern.

With the decline of glass-making in the Levant the scene changes to Italy. The shores of the Venetian lagoons provided, in sand and kelp (for soda), two of the essentials of the craft, and Venice or the neighbouring island of Murano, to which, owing to the danger of fire in the crowded city, the glass-blowers were confined from the thirteenth century onwards, has been from the Middle Ages until to-day its most famous European centre.

Before the fifteenth century, however, the output seems to have consisted only of window-glass, " white " (that is to say, colourless) and coloured, beads, and vessels in plain glass for ordinary use. The Venetians gained one great advantage over mediæval glassmakers in other parts of Europe by discovering how to produce a colourless transparent " metal " which, from its likeness to rock-crystal, they called *cristallo*. Venice glass begins to be important in the history of art only on the eve of the Renaissance, when the process of enamelling already practised by Italian goldsmiths was adapted for painting on glass; the impetus doubtless came from the desire to emulate wares imported from the East, but no evidence has yet been brought to light to prove that the Venetians learned the technique directly from Oriental masters of it. The earliest examples of the new art in Venice date from about the third quarter of the fifteenth century (Plate XV, c); they consist of goblets in coloured glass—blue, green or amethyst—painted with allegorical subjects such as the "Triumphs" of Petrarch forming a continuous frieze round the bowl, or, where betrothal or wedding gifts were intended, with portrait heads of the lovers in medallions separated by foliage. The shapes are those of contemporary metalwork, entirely Gothic in character; the same strong forms persisted till the end of the century (Plate XV, A). Colourless glass then began to be employed in preference to coloured, and the enamelling tended to follow certain stereotyped designs, such as horizontal bands or overlapping scales rendered in small spots of various colours, set off by

PLATE XV

A. Glass cup, Venetian
(British Museum)
(*Page* 142)

B (bottom, left). Glass beaker,
Netherlandish

C (bottom, right). Glass beaker,
Venetian
(*Page* 142)

(B, C, Victoria and Albert Museum)

gilt bands having patterns picked out in them with a
needle-point.

Noble as they are, these earliest Venetian glasses
departed little in form from the types set by the gold-
and silversmith; emancipation came, with advance in
skill and understanding of the material, soon after the
beginning of the sixteenth century. From this time on

Fig. 15.—Wine-glass, Venetian (Victoria and Albert Museum)

for a hundred years and more the Venetians were the
supreme masters of glass-blowing technique; favoured
by a soft readily fusible "metal", they almost excelled
their Roman forerunners in the ease and sureness with
which they guided their ductile material into frail
ethereal shapes of endless variety and consummate loveliness. Vessels of many kinds were fashioned out of the
bubble on their blowing-irons, but the wine-glass on its
slender stem, now for the first time receiving the shape
which has ever since been accepted as most appropriate, is the typical exponent of their skill (fig. 15).

Often the form itself is its only adornment, the members passing into one another without the angular divisions of the earlier goblets; if decoration is added, it consists of one or two simple fillets round the bowl or foot, perhaps in blue, the only colour admitted at this stage. The bowl in its delicate tenuity suggests comparison with a flower, and the petals of flowers are hardly more diverse than the varieties of subtle curve given to its outline; the stem as a rule is composed of a slim baluster separated by one or two rounded knops or collars ("mereses", in glass-blowers' language) from the bowl. Towards the end of the sixteenth century there was a departure from this classical simplicity. Moulds were brought into use for producing ribs on the bowl or reliefs of festoons and lion-masks on the baluster; the stem was often flanked by wing-like or cockscomb ornaments pinched into serrations by deft work with the pincers. The fancy of the craftsmen manipulating the plastic " metal " in its viscous state was given free rein in the creation of all kinds of grotesque and extravagant shapes; birds, flowers, fishes, ships were amongst the forms which the obedient substance was made to endue. The movement went on step by step with the advance in taste from the classical austerity of the High Renaissance to the somewhat bombastic complexities of seventeenth-century Baroque.

Though basing their technique principally on the unrivalled ductility of their *cristallo*, the Venetians made experiments in every direction, retrieving nearly all the processes discovered in Roman times, and since to a large extent forgotten. The opaque white enamel obtained by mixing tin in the metal which had been only sparingly used by their predecessors, they exploited in every possible way under the name of " milk-glass " (*lattimo* or *latticinio*). In the form of bands or fine threads they used it with admirable effect to make vertical white stripes on bottles and drinking-vessels; by twisting these threads or laying them dia-

gonally across one another they produced all manner
of network and filigree patterns. In the eighteenth
century jugs, plates and even tea- and coffee-cups and
saucers were made entirely in this white " metal " in
competition with porcelain, and were, like porcelain,
often painted in enamel colours; a set, now dispersed
in various collections, of white plates with views of
Venice in red monochrome was bought and brought
to England by Horace Walpole. Glass was made to
imitate the markings of semi-precious stones like
jasper and chalcedony; examples of this type were
in the possession of King Henry VIII at Westminster.
An effect unknown to the Romans was that of avan-
turine glass, the surface of which was spangled with
metallic sheen by rolling the heated bubble of glass
in copper filings; another new type, invented in the
sixteenth century, was ice-glass, made by plunging
the heated bubble in water and then reheating it and
blowing it again so as to fuse and distend the cracks
thereby caused on its surface. The only important
process not employed at Venice until the eighteenth
century was that of cutting, to which the Venetian
type of " metal " did not lend itself; engraving with
a diamond was also less often practised at Venice than
elsewhere.

In spite of very severe penalties for desertion imposed by their rulers, the Venetian glass-blowers from
time to time emigrated beyond the Alps, and glass of
the Venetian type (*façon de Venise*) was made in the
sixteenth and seventeenth centuries in several other
countries. Amongst their rivals were a colony of glass-
makers, originally from France, settled since the
Middle Ages at Altare, near Genoa, whose statutes
provided for sending out representatives periodically
to ply their craft in other lands. In the Netherlands
glass of the Venetian kind was made from about 1550
onwards, first at Antwerp, then at Amsterdam, Brussels,
and, by an offshoot from the last-named city, at Liége,

which continues to the present day to be one of the greatest centres of the industry. In the Austrian Tyrol a glasshouse was started in 1534 at Hall, near Innsbruck, and came under the protection of the Archduke Ferdinand. In Germany glasses were made at Cassel which were formerly often mistaken for Venetian; this Hessian glasshouse, which seems to have had only a very short existence towards the end of the sixteenth century, made especially wine-glasses with tall stems composed of cord-like rods, often enclosing twisted white enamel threads, which are contorted into elaborate and sometimes rather formless figures spreading out sideways into pincered ornaments recalling the head and comb of a cock. Effective use was also made of vertical white stripes in the Venetian manner for the decoration of beer-tankards and beakers. Tall glasses with square facets moulded in relief and outlined with white enamel spots were, in the sixteenth century, a speciality of the Spessart district, near Darmstadt. Of the penetration of Venetian glassmaking to England something will be said on a later page.

In Germany, as we have seen, Roman traditions endured until in the Middle Ages the art had sunk to the level of a humble craft, carried on in forest regions where there was a copious supply of wood fuel and producing wares with no pretensions to refinement. The " metal ", in which the alkaline constituent was provided by potash obtained by burning wood (in particular beech), is transparent but of a greenish tone given by a strong iron content uncounteracted by any decolouring agent. This unavoidable green hue is admirably suited to the sturdy shapes of the mediæval vessels and was doubtless deliberately intensified. The characteristic form for this " forest glass " (*Waldglas*), as it was called, is a beaker or jar of slightly bulging outline with flaring top and a pincered frill round the base (Plate XVI, B); it is generally orna-

mented with rows of applied pads drawn out upwards
into a point, or studded with smaller spine-like pro-
jections, the appearance being that of a cabbage stem
with the stumps of stalks from which the leaves have
fallen away. From this form of beaker was developed
the typical German wine-glass, the *Roemer*; this has a
convex bowl, stout shaft studded with raspberry
" prunts " like those of the early Islamic bowls, and
high-spreading foot skilfully made of a thread of glass
in constantly widening coil (as time went on the process was simplified by winding the thread round a
wooden cone and at last, in modern imitations, by
substituting for the spiral a series of narrow contiguous
rings produced by blowing the foot into a corrugated
mould). In both colour and shape these early German
drinking-glasses have great æsthetic merits which
assured their continuance in favour long after more
refined fashions had penetrated the country from
abroad.

In the sixteenth century the wealthy citizens of
South Germany drew large supplies of fine glass from
Venice, including enamelled glasses which were often
painted to order with the arms of the purchasers. In
due course the art of enamelling was itself introduced
into the German glasshouses; it was the more readily
adopted because the type of glass made in Germany
was much harder and less fusible than the Venetian,
lending itself much less readily to plastic treatment.
From about 1550 onwards until well into the eighteenth
century great quantities of painted glass were made in
several parts of the country; the chief centres of production were the forest regions, along both sides of
the mountain chains dividing Bohemia from Bavaria
in one direction and Silesia in another; Kreussen made
glass with designs in some cases almost identical with
those painted, perhaps in the same workshops, on the
stoneware which has already been mentioned (p. 38).
Saxony and Hesse were amongst other districts which

Emperor Rudolph II. At this sovereign's court at
Prague gem-cutting and the carving of semi-precious
stones enjoyed high favour. Lehmann conceived the
idea of extending from rock crystal to glass the technique of wheel-engraving. Glasses engraved by him
are rare. From comparison with his signed works and
on grounds of internal evidence it has been possible
to identify as his also three panes in the Victoria and
Albert Museum; two of these bear dates (1619, 1620),
whilst the third with the subject of Perseus and Andro-
meda displays shields with the initials of Christian II,
Elector of Saxony, and Princess Hedwig of Denmark,
and was doubtless occasioned by their marriage in 1602.
The imperial privilege for glass-engraving granted to
Lehmann was bequeathed by him to his assistant
Georg Schwanhardt, who moved from Prague to
Nuremberg, where he died in 1667. At the latter city
Schwanhardt established a school of glass-engraving
which was carried on under his son and others into
the eighteenth century. These artists decorated with
their engraving covered goblets of an elegant form,
with tall stem composed of tiers of hollow rounded
knops separated by flat discs, which seems to have been
peculiar to Nuremberg; sometimes the bowl and foot
of these goblets were in emerald-green glass and the
stem colourless, as in an example at South Kensington
with engraving attributed to Hermann Schwinger, who
died in 1683.

The improvement in the " metal " by the increase
in its lime content, referred to above, provided an excellent medium for the engraver's art. The new mode of
decoration found ready adoption in the glasshouses
of Bohemia and from there it soon spread to all parts
of Germany; it was not, however, till the last quarter of
the seventeenth century that it was brought in the
Bohemian region to the high level of execution reached
by Schwanhardt and his followers. In Silesia a refinement of the technique was invented in the form of high-

PLATE XVI

A. Engraved glass beaker
(*Page* 153)

B. Green glass beaker, German
(*Page* 146)

(A, B, C, Victoria and Albert Museum)

C. Sweetmeat-glass, cut glass,
English
(*Page* 165)

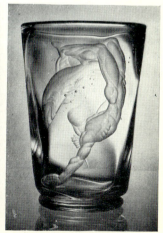

D. Engraved glass beaker,
Swedish (Orrefors)
(*Page* 171)

relief cutting in the manner of a cameo, on goblets blown expressly to an unusual thickness; for these, heavy baroque scroll foliage was the chosen theme, the resemblance to carved rock crystal being here particularly apparent.   About 1700 Bohemia began to take the lead with engraving of fine quality which won deserved renown all over Europe.   Scattered flowers and swags of fruit, or the characteristic baroque scrolls and strapwork for which the fashion was spread by German books of ornament based on the designs of the great French engraver Jean Bérain, were combined with small figure-subjects or landscape scenes of endless variety. The goblets which more especially were chosen for this kind of embellishment were very different in form from those of Nuremberg; dominant amongst them was a bowl with profile recalling a thistle-flower on a solid faceted baluster stem.   In the second quarter of the century Silesia came to the fore with glasses on which designs were engraved on shapes previously cut with faceting carried from the stem right up to the lip, in the form of flat gadroons like the staves of a tub.   A pretty speciality of Silesia was the sweetmeat-glass with baluster stem and boat-shaped bowl cut at one end into a shell-like poop curling inward at the apex. It is interesting to note also that already in this period " presents from " this, that and the other wateringplace were made for sale to visitors, notably at Warmbrunn, which possessed an excellent glassworks as well as a spa.

The art introduced by Lehmann quickly spread to other glass-making districts throughout Germany besides Bohemia and Silesia.   The foremost exponent of relief cutting was Franz Gundelach, who from 1694 onwards worked in glass as well as semi-precious stones at Cassel, in a workshop established by the Landgrave of Hesse;   he carved mythological and other figuresubjects with wonderful refinement of detail on the bowls of goblets, the stems and covers of which he enriched with massive acanthus foliage and gadroons, in the sumptuous baroque manner of the period. At Nuremberg the art was carried on by Anton Mäuerl (1672–1737), who has a special significance from the fact that he worked between 1699 and 1710 in London. As no glass decorated by his hand has as yet been identified in England, it is possible that Mäuerl earned his livelihood whilst in London chiefly by another art of which he was master, that of paper-cutting; but it is not unreasonable to suppose that English glass-cutting is indebted to him as one of its founders. Another contact with England was at the Lauenstein factory, in the duchy of Brunswick, founded in 1701, where amongst other foreign hands was employed one from England belonging to the Tisac or Tyzack family (see p. 160), and the English practice was employed of firing the furnaces with coal.

A very important part was played by the glass-house established in 1674 under the patronage of the Elector of Brandenburg (the "Grosser Kurfürst", Frederick William) at Drewitz, near Potsdam, whence it was moved five years later to the immediate neighbourhood of the residence-town. The high position taken by the Potsdam glasshouse was due to the distinguished scientist, Johann Kunckel, by whom for several years it was directed. Kunckel brought to practical fruition the abortive discovery of another experimenter, Andreas Cassius; this consisted in staining glass to a ruby red by means of chloride of gold ("purple of Cassius"). This ruby glass was the pride of the Brandenburg factory and was employed to make a great variety of goblets, beakers, vases and bottles; these were decorated either with pincered longitudinal ribs, admirably setting off their dignified baroque forms, or with engraved designs. Their effect was sometimes enhanced with gilt mountings added to them at Augsburg. Glass was made by Kunckel in several other colours besides ruby. He also supplied glass of fine quality for the workshop in Berlin of Martin Winter, who was appointed glass-cutter and engraver to the Elector in 1680. Winter took into partnership his nephew Gottfried Spiller. Characteristic of their work are mythological and other figure-subjects, cut in deep intaglio, carried round the whole circumference of a beaker or vase; massive covered beakers with bacchanalian *putti*, to be seen in the Victoria and Albert Museum, are attributed to the senior and junior partners respectively (Plate XVI, A). Another interesting glass at South Kensington, with allegorical subjects relating to the Treaty of Lund, between Sweden and Denmark (1679), bears the signature of a pupil of Spiller, Heinrich Jäger.

Amongst the numerous other local variations of technique devised in Germany one or two call for special mention, as examples of them are often to be met with in museums. Enamel painting was brought to a special degree of fineness by various artists who in this way decorated in their private workshops not only glass but also fine earthenware and at a later stage porcelain as well. The earliest of these fine enamellers was Johann Schaper, who settled at Nuremberg in 1655 and died in 1670. His style was a development of the Dutch window-painting of the sixteenth and seventeenth centuries, and he himself actually painted window glass, both in leaded panels and in single " monolith " panes; a pane with the Crucifixion in black monochrome, in the Victoria and Albert Museum, bears his initials and is dated *Regensburg*, 1655 (Schaper is recorded as having been at Ratisbon about that time). This black painting (*Schwarzlotmalerei*) he afterwards used extensively for the decoration of drinking-glasses, chiefly small cylindrical goblets resting on three depressed balls and having a domed lid with multiple knob. His manner is as delicate as that of the miniature portrait-painter. For his subjects he chose most frequently landscapes with ruins, often a fountain and small figures, all rendered in minute detail. Schaper was followed in his peculiar art by others such as Hermann Benchertt and Johann Ludwig Faber, signed examples of whose work may be seen in London museums.

In the middle of the eighteenth century another technique was invented in some locality hitherto unidentified in Bohemia; its frequent employment for rendering sacred subjects, in addition to the hunting-scenes which were also favoured, makes it likely that its practitioners were amateurs belonging to some monastic community. The process consisted in scratching designs through gold leaf and encasing them between two layers of glass, in the manner of those of the early Christian medallions (see p. 133), but by an essentially different technique; whilst these latter were fixed by fusing over them an outer layer of transparent glass, the *Zwischengoldgläser*, as they are called, are small conical tumblers with double walls. The inner wall has the gilt design, in silhouette with scratched details, on the outside, the outer wall is ground to fit exactly over it and cut externally with longitudinal faceting, and the one overlaps the other at the top and is secured inside it by means of an unfired adhesive. A disc made separately and fixed under the base of the inner glass is often washed over on its upper surface with translucent pink or green lacquer, so that the gilt design inside the base of the glass is seen against a coloured background.

CHAPTER III

Spain, France, and England

SPAIN and France have played a less conspicuous part in the evolution of glass than Italy, Germany, or even England. In Spain a tradition stretching back through the period of Arab domination to Roman times has continued to the present day in the production of glass with a soda content, in the form of vessels for ordinary use with decoration, where present, obtained solely by manipulation of the metal in its soft condition, before cooling. The typical Spanish wares are quite unlike those of any other land, as may be seen by a study of the small but representative collection at South Kensington. The material is more or less strongly stained with iron, varying from bluish green and brownish olive to horn colour. The typical vessels are jugs and two-handled vases with bulbous body and wide flaring neck often pinched into wavy lobes at the top, the sprinkler with ring handle at the top and two spouts—one wide for filling, the other long and narrow for sprinkling—rising vertically from the shoulder, and the peculiar conical wine-jar with long tapering spout for pouring a thin jet of liquor into the open mouth of the drinker. These vessels often display a typically Spanish exuberance in their multiplicity of handles with serrated spines and the applied frills and threads with which by means of the pincers they are ornamented. Precise classification by locality is difficult, as glass of this order was made in many parts of Spain, but Almeria, on the coast of Andalusia, with its Islamic past, was a leading producer.

Another centre of production was in Catalonia. At Barcelona, and at Cadalso in Castile, where an off-shoot of the Catalan industry was established, Venetian methods took root in the fifteenth and sixteenth centuries, and glass was made which is sometimes not easy to distinguish from the Venetian. Opaque white threads, either as plain bands or in filigree twists, were much employed for decoration, and one un-mistakable class of Barcelona glass shows designs of running animals, birds and fronds painted in a peculiar scheme of enamel colours, chiefly green, yellow and white. In the eighteenth century the native types of glass seem to have passed out of favour except amongst the lower orders, and a factory was set up under royal patronage for competing with the fashions of northern Europe; after a short career elsewhere this was located from 1728 onwards at La Granja de San Ildefonso, near Segovia. Here colourless glass was made, with engraved designs, often picked out with gilding, in which Bohemian and Netherlandish in-fluences are clearly apparent.

In France, from the Middle Ages onwards, there has been a vast production of glass, particularly of window-glass and latterly of mirrors, but little has been made in the way of vessels with decorative qualities. Nor-mandy and Lorraine in particular have both supplied large quantities of wares, and have sent forth glass-blowers, sometimes to escape from religious persecu-tion, to ply their craft in England and other countries. In the middle of the sixteenth century, in some locality not yet identified with certainty, enamel painting in the Venetian manner was practised; a typical example, in the Buckley Gift at South Kensington, has figures of a man and woman in the dress of gentry of the period, in red, blue, white and gold, and the words *IE SVIS A VOUS*, *Ferme cueur côtre fortune*. It was perhaps brought to England when it was made, as an inscription scratched on it with a diamond in seventeenth century handwriting tells us that it was " found in a hole behind the ivy in Stoke Courci Castle " (Stogursey, near Taunton), which was destroyed in the Civil Wars. In the seventeenth century, a glasshouse was established at Nevers by the duke, Louis de Gonzague, with workmen from Altare, which was in one of his Italian domains; here amongst other things were made little figures of coloured glass which were sometimes combined in elaborate groups to represent subjects such as the Nativity and the Crucifixion. None of these French ventures was of any great importance; it was not until the latter part of the nineteenth century that France made any effective contribution to the art, in the work of an artist to be mentioned in the next chapter.

The Netherlands were remarkable not so much for their large output of glass as for certain modes of decoration there practised with pre-eminent skill. Mention has already been made (p. 145) of the glasshouses working on Venetian lines which were established in several cities, notably at Liége. On the whole, Liége glass, apart from the earlier wares made in the Venice fashion, lacks originality of form and is not in other ways noteworthy. Much of the great quantity produced there in the eighteenth century approximates in shape to the English glass of the period, but is inferior to it in quality. Holland, on the other hand, is peculiar for the great cult of glass-engraving which sprang up during the great days of Dutch prosperity in the seventeenth century and lasted well into the nineteenth. The art was to a large extent practised not on a commercial footing, but as a pastime by amateurs, many of whom were poets and other persons of literary tastes. The tool employed was a diamond point; wheel-engraving in the Bohemian manner was a later introduction, and was never brought in Holland

to the highest level of attainment. In diamond engraving the Dutch stand unsurpassed. As recipients
for their skilful exercises the engravers employed both
home-made and foreign glasses. Some of the Dutch
wine-glasses in the Venetian manner of the second
half of the seventeenth century (it may here be said
in parenthesis) are quite admirable in their simple
gracefulness of form; the dominant types show a bowl
either bucket-shaped or conical—sometimes drawn out
to the high narrow form known as a flute—and a
hollow baluster stem either pear-shaped or of a slender,
elegant spindle shape. When English lead glass (see
p. 162) became available it soon began to make its way
to Holland, and many of the later engraved glasses are
undoubtedly importations from England—in some
cases it would seem made specially in shapes to suit
the Dutch taste. At the same time it is no surprise
to learn that with the help of English workmen the
Dutch took to making lead glass for themselves; Mr.
Francis Buckley, to whose unflagging industry in
research historians of English glass are so deeply indebted, has discovered an advertisement in a Man-
chester newspaper of 1739 which—quite apart from
other evidence—puts this fact, long a matter of dis-
pute amongst students of the subject, virtually beyond
doubt.

The earliest Dutch diamond-engraved glasses are
unsigned; the oldest with a date is of 1581, and a
well-known beaker in the Rÿksmuseum, Amsterdam,
with a satirical subject after a German engraving—
Christ confronting the Pope—is dated 1604. To this
period belong several *Roemers* (see p. 147), such as one
of green glass in the Victoria and Albert Museum engraved with the arms of the seven United Provinces.
The earliest of the amateur engravers to sign their
names were the literary ladies, Anna Roemers Visscher
(b. 1583, d. 1651), and her younger sister, Maria Tes-
selschade. The glasses they chose to work on were

mostly green *Roemers*; for their motives they sometimes copied birds, insects and flowers from contemporary books on natural history, but their great achievement was the adaptation to glass of inscriptions in
the swinging scrolled lettering, popularized by the calli-
graphers of the time. The engraving of glasses with this
calligraphic ornament was adopted also as a diversion
by Willem Jacobsz van Heemskerk (1613–92), a cloth
manufacturer of Leyden. Amongst many other clever
exponents of the art was Mooleyser of Rotterdam, of
whom little is known beyond what can be learned from
his signature inscribed on glasses such as a beaker
dated 1685, with frolicking drinkers and vine-stems, at
South Kensington.

For rendering light and shade in details of her subjects Anna Visscher sometimes employed, instead of
lines, thickly clustered spots made by pressing the
point of the diamond vertically into the surface of the
glass. This procedure was taken up by a later artist,
Frans Greenwood, an amateur, born of English parents
at Rotterdam. All the dated glasses with his signature
except the earliest are engraved entirely in stipple, that
is, the designs are done in myriads of tiny dots hammered
into the glass with a diamond point; the dated examples
of this technique range from 1722 to 1755. For his
subjects Greenwood for the most part drew upon
engravings after genre and allegorical pictures by
Dutch masters, which he freely adapted to his purposes. His technique had many imitators, none of
whom was more skilful than David Wolff, born at
Bois-le-Duc. His latest dated glass on record is of
1796; his subjects are mostly portraits, of the Stad-
holder William V and others, or children in allegorical
compositions. This Dutch stipple engraving is in
the nature of a *tour de force*, not to be criticized too
seriously as a means of decoration; the cloudy film,
almost as ethereal as breath on a cold pane, with which
it overlays the surface, is a curiosity which begins to

have a meaning only when on close inspection it is
found to be a picture. The technique was hardly possible except on the soft unresistant metal of lead glass,
and many of the glasses employed to receive it, notably
those with drawn stem (often cut in facets) chosen by
Wolff, are almost certainly of English manufacture (it
is known that there was a considerable export of glass
to Holland from Newcastle-on-Tyne).

In England, as elsewhere in northern Europe, glass-
blowing in the Middle Ages was a humble craft, making
vessels for use only, in a metal strongly tinged with
green, and carried on in woodland regions like the
Weald of Surrey and Sussex, where a plentiful supply
was at hand of timber and fern to burn for potash.
It was only when fine glass began to come in quantities
from Venice in Tudor times that any efforts were
made to compete in quality with the imported wares
by setting up a manufacture of the same order in
England. Various ventures are recorded, such as a
short-lived settlement of Venetians in London in the
middle of the sixteenth century, and the introduction
of glass-workers from Lorraine about twenty years
later by John Carr or Carré of Antwerp. The Lorrainers
migrated from their first adopted home in Sussex in
pursuit of the requisite fuel to various other woodland
districts such as the Forest of Dean, and thence north-
wards to the coalfields; their descendants, with names
of French derivation such as Tyzack (compare p. 152)
and Henzey or Ensell, originated the modern glass
industries of Stourbridge and Newcastle-on-Tyne.
Nothing certain is known of the products of these
immigrant glass-makers until we come to a Venetian
named Jacob Verzelini, whose memorial brass may be
seen in the church at Downe, in Kent. Verzelini had
lived in Antwerp, before at some date not established
with certainty he came to London. In 1575 he was
granted by Queen Elizabeth a licence for twenty-one
years for making " drynkinge glasses such as be

accustomablie made in the towne of Morano ". There are several goblets bearing dates from 1577[1] to 1586, which have been plausibly attributed to Verzelini. They have bowls ranging in shape from semi-oviform to a shallow inverted dome, and a hollow knop, variously formed, on the stem, shapes which differ in their proportions, as does the metal by its inferior, somewhat horny quality, from any known to have been made in Venice. One of these goblets has thin horizontal fillets of white enamel and a little gilding; otherwise the decoration of all four consists of engraving with a diamond point comprising inscriptions or initials amongst arabesques, petal-motives, and in one case a frieze of animals. Two of the glasses bear the motto of the Pewterers' Company of the City of London. In certain respects the designs are not unlike those on the *Humpen* made for William Smith of Nuremberg (see p. 149).

The year 1611 is a landmark in the history of the industry, as a patent was then granted for the construction of glass-furnaces to be fired with coal. Seven years later a monopoly of the glass manufacture in England was acquired by Admiral Sir Robert Mansell, who became controller of glasshouses all over the country. Although glass of the Venetian type of *cristallo* continued to be made in England, and as late as about 1670 there was a market in London for glass made to order in Venice in special shapes for English use, the introduction of coal fuelling prepared the way for a revolution which was to give English glass a world-wide supremacy. Coal had before this time been used spasmodically in Germany (compare p. 152), but it was in England that this new practice first brought about an effective change in the quality of the metal produced. The use of coal instead of wood necessitated the substitution of covered for open

---

[1] This date is inscribed on a glass recorded for the first time and reproduced in *Apollo*, XXX, 1939, p. 86.

crucibles, to protect the glass mixture in the furnace from impurities; the loss of heat thus caused prompted the search for a more readily fusible metal, and this, in due course, led to the addition to the ingredients of a large proportion of lead as a flux; English lead glass, commonly known by a trade misnomer as "flint glass", was thereby brought to birth. The nature of the glass made at Greenwich after the Restoration, by Venetians working for the Duke of Buckingham, can only be conjectured (a well-known goblet diamond-engraved with the portraits of Charles II and Queen Catherine and the Royal Oak, dated 1663, is now generally held to be Dutch); the factory was probably occupied chiefly in making mirror-plates. We first arrive at certainty with the advent of George Ravenscroft, who in 1673 set up a glasshouse in the Savoy, in London, and a year later opened another under an agreement with the Glass Sellers' Company at Henley-on-Thames; he engaged to assist him an Italian from Altare (compare p. 145). Experiments conducted by Ravenscroft resulted in the improvement of the metal, obviating a liability to "crissel" or decay, by introducing lead into its composition; the glass of lead ("flint glass") which he invented about 1676 or earlier, has since been the standard English type for table wares.

Like the cream-coloured ware of Wedgwood (see p. 47) English lead glass was destined to capture the markets of Europe and to force imitation of it on competitors abroad. It owes its supreme beauty as a material to its brilliance, and its unrivalled aptitude for reflecting and refracting rays of light; its weight made for stability and dignity of outline, and the sound craftsmanship of English glass at its best atones for any lack of the fancifulness or elaboration of finish belonging to the more ambitious performances of Venice and Bohemia.

Advertisements tell us that Ravenscroft introduced

the use of an applied glass seal with a raven's head in
relief as the mark of his productions. Several specimens still exist—jugs, basins, and drinking-glasses—
which bear this seal and give us some idea of the nature
of his wares. In nearly every case the articles so marked
are of the new metal containing lead. In shape some
of these resemble earthenware vessels of the time,
whilst one is a goblet similar in form to a German
Roemer, with raspberry " prunts "
on the stem. Vertical ribs, sometimes pinched with the tongs into
a diamond trellis in relief, recur
as motives of decoration. From
these earliest products in lead
glass it is possible, with the help
of a few dated or datable examples,
to trace the development of shape
and design down to the nineteenth
century.

The English glass made in the
new " metal " in the period about
the turn of the century continues
to show clear traces of Venetian
influence in shape and decoration.
Goblets often of imposing size
have mostly a straight-sided bowl
rounded at the base, resting on
a well-proportioned stem with a
knop, or perhaps two, above a
baluster. The knops may be lobed

Fig. 16.—Early English wine-
glass (Chequers, Bucks.)

and the bowl surrounded by gadrooning in the lower
part or with nipped trelliswork (fig. 16). Threads trailed
on in loops also occur, and all these features can likewise
be seen in candlesticks, tankards, and covered sweet-
meat-glasses, and in the posset-pots with crown-like knob
on the lid and spiny volute handles which recall similar
pots bearing dates about 1700 in Bristol delft ware
(compare p. 98). As time went on smaller wine-glasses

began to be made, with lighter knopped stem, or with straight stem formed in one piece with the bowl, which is drawn out downwards like a funnel (fig. 17). An innovation consisting of a shouldered stem of square section (sometimes incorrectly called a " Silesian " stem), occasionally moulded with the inscription " God save the King ", had its prototype in Hesse; its introduction is doubtless traceable to the arrival in England of German craftsmen as one of the consequences of the Treaty of Utrecht (1713), though the case of Mäuerl

Fig. 17.—Cordial-glass,
English
(Victoria and Albert
Museum)

already mentioned (p. 152) shows that such immigration was then not without precedent. Of greater moment was the importation of Bohemian engraved glass and at the same time, by German practitioners, of the art of decorative glass-engraving as distinct from the simple shaping and bevelling known to the mirror-manufacturers of the Restoration period. The evolution of shape in the wine-glass at this stage shows the baluster or knopped stem giving way to a perfectly plain column joined with an abrupt angle to the base of the bowl, which takes the form of a trumpet-mouth, a thistle or a bucket. Engraving led on to cutting, and in 1727 we find the first advertisement of " curious cut glass " for sale in London; in 1739 an advertisement gives us definite evidence of an English glass-cutter named Jerom Johnson.

Glass-cutting, the art in which English glass-manufacturers were soon to excel all others, imposing their fashions on foreign competitors, was peculiarly adapted to display the lustrous brilliance of the lead " metal ". It received a great impetus from an entirely extraneous circumstance; in 1745, to raise funds for the war with

France, an Excise Act was passed by Parliament imposing a duty amongst other things on all the materials used in the manufacture of glass. The consequence of this was that the manufacturers found themselves forced to cheapen their wares by making them smaller in size and lighter—by reduction of the proportion of the heavy ingredient, lead—and at the same time to render them more attractive to buyers by a more extensive use of cut decoration (Plate XVI, c). This decoration first took the form chiefly of a diamond-pattern applied to the stem of a wine-glass, the lower part of a decanter, or the whole surface of a cruet-bottle or sugar-basin. It was further elaborated in time to scallops round rim or foot and shallow faceting in great variety, until we come to the hobnail and strawberry-diamond cutting of the beginning of the nineteenth century, followed in turn by the sharp and vulgar over-decoration of the Great Exhibition period. Cutting was used with great effect on chandeliers and table candelabra, on the shaft, arms, sconces, and prismatic lustres and drops. Splendid examples are the six great chandeliers in the Assembly Rooms at Bath, made for the rooms when they were opened in 1771, at the Whitefriars Glasshouse, London, for William Parker, dealer in cut glass, of Fleet Street.

Other means besides cutting and engraving were adopted by the English glass-makers after the passing of the 1745 Act, to make their wares more saleable; one of these was by colouring the " metal ", as may be gathered from the mention of glass " of all colours " in advertisements of 1752 and later. Another was by the introduction of white enamel as a decoration, in the form especially of white twisted threads encased in the stems of wine-glasses; the earliest example on record inscribed with a date is of 1754. These opaque white twists had been preceded by hollow air-twists, which occur for instance in many of the well-known Jacobite glasses made after the rising of 1745 and

engraved with a rose and two buds and other emblems
of the cause; air-twists were evolved from the cluster of
bubbles sometimes pricked as decoration in the knops
of the baluster stems of the early eighteenth century.
In time twists of ruby, green and other colours were
combined with white, until a new Excise Act, in 1777,
dealt a fatal blow at this form of decoration by extending the duty from " flint glass " to " all enamel, stained
or paste glass ", an act which gave fresh encouragement
to the employment of cutting and tended to further
reduction in size. White and other enamel colours were
used also as pigments, notably on Newcastle-on-Tyne
glass decorated by members of the Beilby family about
1760–70. Special mention must be made also of the
coloured and opaque white glass made about this time
at Bristol; Michael Edkins has a deserved reputation
for the porcelain-like white glass bottles, vases and
tea-caddies painted by him in gay colours with flowers,
birds and occasionally Chinese figures. A word may be
said also of the flasks, bottles and jugs with flecks or
streaks of white or coloured enamel made in the factory
carried on from 1788 to 1873 at Nailsea in Somerset.
Its earlier wares were in black or green bottle-glass,
which was less heavily taxed than lead glass; later,
presumably after the repeal of the Excise Acts in
1845, similar decoration was applied to colourless lead
glass.

Glass-making in Ireland followed a course parallel
to that of English glass. Lead glass began to be made
in Dublin about the beginning of the eighteenth century, but it was not till 1745 that the Irish manufacture
became important. The duty leviable by the Excise
Act of that year did not apply to Ireland, which was
thus free to profit by the handicap imposed on the
hitherto large importation of glass from Great Britain.
In the main it may be said that the glass made at
Dublin, Waterford, Cork and elsewhere, largely with
the help of operatives introduced from England, was

similar in general character to contemporary English glass. Exemption from duty accounts for the continued production in Ireland of glass of fine quality, owing its brilliance to an undiminished proportion of lead content. Towards the end of the eighteenth century it became the custom in Ireland to mark with the name of the firm, in relief under the base, decanters blown into a mould. Certain other forms of the same period may also be taken as characteristically Irish, such as dessert-bowls on a detached stand cut with horizontal ridges, and boat-shaped fruit-dishes cut with scallops at the rim and a band of diamond or star pattern, and supported on a rather ungainly high foot heavily moulded either with gadroons or in the form of a square pedestal.

CHAPTER IV

Modern Glass

G LASS like other forms of applied art suffered from the æsthetic stagnation and confusion of aim which was the usual result of industrialization. All manner of technical improvements were introduced such as the use of steam as the motive power for the glass-cutter's wheel, but attention was focused on mechanical efficiency at the expense of artistic quality. In the first half of the nineteenth century the most interesting innovations took place in Bohemia. Coloured glass began to be made in imitation of natural stones, first opaque black and red like marble and porphyry, then in all kinds of colours in combination, streaked to simulate the markings of agate and onyx; these two new types were, in accordance with the fashion of the time, given names of Greek derivation, " hyalith " and " lithyalin ", respectively. About 1830 there began, especially in the works at Haida and Windisch-Kamnitz, an immense production of glass with engraving deeply cut through a thin surface-staining of colour, especially ruby derived from gold (purple of Cassius). Favourite themes for the engraver were subjects relating to the chase and views of romantic scenery, often with titles in Gothic lettering. Bohemian glass of this kind enjoyed a great popularity and was imitated about 1850 by the manufacturers of Birmingham and Stourbridge. The staple English output, however, consisted of colourless cut-glass with patterns in ever more complicated and inappropriate elaboration of those prevalent earlier in the century. Reaction came at last under the influence of John Ruskin, who was misled by the tasteless extravagances of his time into an entire failure to appreciate the æsthetic possibilities of cutting when used with restraint as a means of decorating glass. In 1859 Philip Webb designed for the use of William Morris glasses made at the Whitefriars Works in London which make their appeal solely by their functional form, being entirely undecorated; this reversion to simple blow shapes was maintained in the table glass made about twelve years later from designs by Morris himself and T. G. Jackson. The next movement was the reintroduction by Joseph Brocard of Paris, in the third quarter of the nineteenth century, of enamel painting inspired by the Syrian glass of the Middle Ages with which museums of industrial art, then newly-founded, were making the public acquainted. This lead was quickly followed by the firm of J. and L. Lobmeyr of Vienna and others in Germany; their productions were chiefly adaptations or copies of the native enamelled glass of the seventeenth century.

In all this, however, there was little trace of healthy invention. The Paris Exhibition of 1900 marks a step in advance, with several innovations then being brought to fruition. France again took the lead, with the decorative glass made by Émile Gallé of Nancy, in which floral motives were executed on vases mostly of massive build by grinding away a layer of colour differing from that underlying it (Gallé sometimes also adopted etching with hydrofluoric acid as an auxiliary to grinding). In this technique he was to some extent anticipated by John Northwood and other manufacturers of Stourbridge, who forty years earlier were making cameo glass in the antique style, including a copy of the Portland vase (see p. 132); Gallé was influenced, however, not so much by Roman as by Chinese glass, then a novelty in Europe, in which the same method was adopted. But although his technique recalls the Chinese, Gallé was entirely original in his designs. It may be said here in parenthesis that Chinese glass, as recent research has proved, was of no importance until the seventeenth century; before that time its use was limited to small moulded articles such as the amulets found in graves of the Sung period, and it was not until the reign of Ch'ien Lung (1736–95) that the wheel-cutting of dichromatic or polychrome glass was adopted, as in the snuff-bottles to be seen in most museums of Oriental art.

America in the eighteenth and nineteenth centuries had its glass-works on English lines, such as those of Sandwich, New Jersey, or producing amongst the immigrants in Pennsylvania enamelled glass of the German type. About 1900 a new departure was made by Louis Tiffany, of New York, who discovered a method of producing an iridescent metallic sheen on the surface of his vases by carefully controlled reheating. In Germany at the same time Karl Köpping of Berlin was making vases blown in shapes of ethereal delicacy inspired by the forms of flowers, leaves and tendrils.

The last two decades have witnessed an expansion of glass design and technique, and an ever-widening application of the material to every kind of use such as was never before seen in so short a span of time. To enumerate all recent developments of glass as an art would here be quite impossible. A few only of the outstanding achievements must be mentioned.

In Bohemia and Germany developments have been chiefly in the direction of cutting and engraving. Starting from Neo-classical forms cut faceting has been taken up, at Haida and elsewhere, often with an effect of simple linear elegance. Deep engraving of figure-subjects in a tradition traceable to Gundelach and Spiller (see pp. 151, 153) has been done at Stuttgart by Wilhelm von Eiff and his associates and by Ena

Rottenberg and other artists working for J. & L. Lobmeyr of Vienna, and the daughter firm of Stein-schönau, in Bohemia. The figure-engraving done by Richard Süssmuth at Penzig, in Silesia, sometimes on glass with one or more superficial coloured layers, is restrained within the limits of an austere linear styliza-tion suggested by ancient Roman precedents. Bohem-ian technical traditions have been widely effective in other countries also. In America they are the basis of the productions of the Steuben Glassworks at Cor-ning, New York, where an adapted Neo-classicism is dominant; but modern Swedish glass is the most remarkable offshoot from the same stock. In Sweden, artistic glass of the finest quality and in great variety of design has been made during the last twenty years, notably since 1917 in the works at Orrefors, near Kalmar (Plate XVI, D), and in the Kosta glasshouse, an eighteenth-century foundation. The artists who led this revival are Simon Gate and Edvard Hald. The engraving of the former tends to overspin the surface with formal designs peopled with small figures, of an airy elegance in keeping with the trend—again with a distinct savour of the neo-classical—which has recently dominated Swedish architecture and applied arts; Hald chooses by preference the nude figure, treated with the exuberance of the German baroque glass-engravers. The Swedish glassworks have also been making glass with little or no added decoration, owing its effect solely to the formal and luminous qualities of the material itself, or to studied grading of tone where the " metal " has been coloured. From Sweden Bohemian influences and technique have been passed on in turn to the English glass-works; this is apparent in the designs of Keith Murray, working for Stevens and Williams of Stourbridge, and in the productions of the Whitefriars factory of James Powell & Sons, removed in 1923 from its ancient site in London to Harrow. The fireproof table wares made at

Smethwick and Sunderland show a fine sense of form in their severely functional shapes.

In France there has been a great blossoming of the art since the beginning of the century. The path opened up by Émile Gallé has been followed by René Lalique, the champion of uncoloured glass, and François Décorchemont, who have specialized in decoration stamped or moulded in high relief, sometimes helped out with engraving, intended to display the beauties of glass as glass. The visual kinship of glass with rock crystal has inspired other French artists such as Aristide Colotte of Nancy to use it in great blocks for solid sculpture, brusquely carved so as to give the most effective play of reflected light. Maurice Marinot, working at Bar-sur-Seine, shows a preference for very massive glass blown in the swelling shapes he claims as characteristic of the blower's art; similarly heavy forms are chosen by Henri Navarre, who spangles his glass with metallic colours. Floral design in enamel applied in strong relief or etched with acid are amongst the distinctive productions of Paul Daum, of Nancy.

Venice has played a somewhat subordinate part in the modern movement. The revival of glass-blowing at Murano in 1838, fostered later by Antonio Salviati, produced at first nothing better than skilful but lifeless reproductions of the styles of the great age of Venetian glass-blowing, degenerating into vulgar and tasteless exhibitions of clever craftsmanship. In recent years, however, the essential qualities of blown glass and the peculiar beauties attainable with colouring oxides have been exploited by the firms of Venini and Barovier, in a manner more worthy of a city acknowledged in earlier times as the unrivalled mistress of the art.

INDEX